Improving inclusive innovation outcomes

Lessons from post-industrial and post-conflict cities

Michael R. Glass, Louise Kempton,
David Marlow, Luke Green,
Carlos Cadena-Gaitan, Sabina Deitrick
and Diana Morales

Regional Studies Policy Impact Books
Series Editor: Louise Kempton

Routledge
Taylor & Francis Group
LONDON AND NEW YORK

RSA Regional Studies Association
Research Today, Policy Tomorrow

i3O
improving inclusive innovation outcomes

First published 2027
by Taylor & Francis
4 Park Square, Milton Park, Abingdon, Oxon, OX14 4RN

Taylor & Francis Group, an informa business

British Library Cataloguing-in-Publication Data
A catalogue record for this book is available from the British Library.

ISBN13: 978-1-041-34193-2 (print)
ISBN13: 978-1-003-79153-9 (e-book)

DOI: 10.4324/9781003791539

Typeset in 10.5/13.5 Myriad Pro
by Nova Techset Private Limited, Bengaluru and Chennai, India

Disclosure statement: No potential conflict of interest was reported by the authors.
Please visit https://taylorandfrancis.com/about/corporate-responsibility/accessibility-at-taylor-francis/ for further information on the accessibility features available for Regional Studies Policy Impact Books

For Product Safety Concerns and Information please contact our EU representative: GPSR@taylorandfrancis.com Taylor & Francis Verlag GmbH, Kaufingerstraße 24, 80331 München, Germany.

CONTENTS

Acknowledgements

The authors acknowledge the invaluable contributions of the many community organisations and representatives, and the policy partners in Belfast, Medellín, Newcastle upon Tyne and Pittsburgh who kindly offered their insights and expertise. Special thanks to our university colleagues at Queen's University Belfast, EAFIT University in Medellín, Newcastle University and the University of Pittsburgh, and especially to Dr Gainbi Park for producing the maps that appear in Chapter 4.

The ideas in this book were developed through rich and informative discussions at Regional Studies Association (RSA) conferences in Ljubljana (June 2023), Florence (June 2024) Porto (May 2025) and London (November 2024 and 2025).

Thanks to Tom Merriweather at the RSA for his support of this book project; and to Emil Evenhuis at the PBL Netherlands Environmental Assessment Agency for his editorial oversight in bringing the manuscript to publication.

The authors also gratefully acknowledge the financial support provided by the RSA through its Policy Expo grant scheme, which made this research possible, and the support of the UK Economic and Social Research Council (ESRC) Impact Acceleration Account [grant number ES/X004449/1]. We are indebted to Third Life Economics for its significant investments, which ensured the work maintained its policy focus at every stage.

https://doi.org/10.1080/2578711X.2025.2624316

About the authors

Michael R. Glass is an Assistant Professor of Sociology and Director of the Urban Studies Program at the University of Pittsburgh. glass@pitt.edu. https://orcid.org/0000-0003-3522-1519

Louise Kempton is Professor of Urban and Regional Policy and Director of the Center for Urban and Regional Development Studies (CURDS) at Newcastle University, UK. louise.kempton@newcastle.ac.uk. https://orcid.org/0000-0002-4684-5565

David Marlow is Chief Executive of Third Life Economics and Visiting Professor of Practice at Newcastle University, UK. davidmarlow@thirdlifeeconomics.co.uk. https://orcid.org/0000-0001-6970-6798

Luke Green is a Research Associate at Insights North East, and holds a doctorate from Newcastle University, UK. luke.green@newcastle.ac.uk. https://orcid.org/0009-0006-2813-4723

Carlos Cadena-Gaitan is an Associate Professor of Policy and Development at EAFIT University, Medellín. ccadena3@eafit.edu.co. https://orcid.org/0000-0003-2634-9262

Sabina Deitrick is an Associate Professor and Co-Director of the Urban and Regional Program at the University Center for Social and Urban Research (UCSUR) at the University of Pittsburgh. sabinad@pitt.edu. https://orcid.org/0000-0003-0977-3395

Diana Morales is University Assistant (postdoctoral) at the Department of Geography and Regional Research at the University of Vienna. diana.carolina.morales.arcila@univie.ac.at. https://orcid.org/0000-0001-6277-2784

https://doi.org/10.1080/2578711X.2025.2624950

Foreword 1

There is now a consensus that innovation is vital for growth. Yet the distributional consequences of innovation create a major challenge, as the benefits of innovation-led growth can be unevenly distributed.

Urban innovation districts sit at the focal points of this tension. They combine close proximity to often deprived, formerly industrial, neighbourhoods and dense concentrations of innovation-intensive firms, research institutes and other actors. As a result, they both reveal the conflicts that innovation can create and also provide a testbed for potential solutions.

How can policymakers balance the need for innovation with the need for inclusion? This book, written by a world-leading group of policy-focused academics and practitioners, offers a route for policymakers wanting to address this question. Based on four detail-rich case studies, it provides a toolkit to understand inclusive innovation activity in innovation districts.

The book makes both conceptual and practical contributions. It offers a new definition of inclusive innovation based on the co-creation of new ideas, practices and technologies. But it also helps apply this model through the "i3o model" – a toolkit to show how policymakers can adapt the learnings of these four case studies to their own local circumstances. Such context-sensitive models avoid naive policy replication, but give policymakers structure and guidance based on what has worked elsewhere.

Yet perhaps the most important aspect of the book is that it shows that innovation and equity need not be in tension. By including workers from across deprived neighbourhoods who come from different backgrounds, efforts to make innovation more inclusive can result in more innovation overall. This book can help make this happen.

Neil Lee
Professor of Economic Geography Department of Geography and Environment London School of Economics, UK
n.d.lee@lse.ac.uk

https://doi.org/10.1080/2578711X.2025.2624317

Foreword 2

This book arrives at a moment when many cities – especially in Latin America – are confronting the limits of traditional innovation models. From my work in Medellín, Colombia, a city that has wrestled with how to place inclusion at the centre of its innovation narrative, I recognise in this study a combination of intellectual knowledge and practical guidance.

What the authors achieve here is to make visible the tensions that shape innovation districts: the struggle between growth and equity, the fragility of governance coalitions, and the lived consequences for communities that are too often treated as spectators rather than partners. The comparative analysis offers something valuable to policymakers and urban innovators: a framework for designing systems that are not only competitive but also socially anchored and legitimate.

This book matters because it reminds us that innovation is not an abstract aspiration – it is something that unfolds in real spaces, with real people, and with real and complex power dynamics. For those of us committed to building more just and inclusive systems, it offers both clarity and hope.

Ana María Ortega
Full Professor and Researcher, Innovation Systems and Community-Based Adaptation (CBA), EAFIT University, Medellín; Policy Advisor, Entrepreneurship and Regional Innovation Systems
aortega1@eafit.edu.co

https://doi.org/10.1080/2578711X.2025.2624320

Preface: The origins of i3o: a story of splendid serendipity

Before you start reading this book, we thought it was important to give some background on how the Improving Inclusive Innovation Outcomes (i3o) project, now a growing collaborative endeavour of more than three years' standing, came about. The i3o experience highlights what many discover during their careers: the importance of serendipitous encounters, which often happen in spaces curated by organisations such as the Regional Studies Association (RSA); how (relatively) modest amounts of funding support can have a transformational impact in achieving significant research and policy impact; and how finding your academic "tribe" can be equally game-changing in terms of accelerating and deepening a previously solo endeavour.

One of the most important questions any "academic tribe" must answer is the "so what?" question for their major research endeavours. The principle that the most important outcome of major research programmes should be actionable insights for policymaking is something shared deeply across our team, who collectively have decades of professional experience in local, regional and international development, planning, research and policy. We hope the goals of asking "so what?" to answer "then what?" are reflected in both this book and with the wider outcomes of the i3o programme.

WHERE IT ALL BEGAN

Figure 0.1 was taken at the entrance to the Helix, Newcastle upon Tyne's innovation district located on the site of the former Newcastle Brewery (erstwhile home to the famed Brown Ale). We will not go into detail about the Helix as this is well covered in this book. What is important to note from this image are the two buildings. First is that on the left, named the Catalyst, built at a cost of £50 million, home to several national innovation centres, highly innovative businesses and filled with lots of bright people doing innovative things on data and ageing.

https://doi.org/10.1080/2578711X.2025.2624321

Figure 0.1 The Helix innovation district in Newcastle upon Tyne, with the Catalyst building on the left and The People's Kitchen in the historic building on the right.

Photo: Louise Kempton, September 2019

But even more important is the historic brick building on the right: The People's Kitchen. It was established in 1985 by a local woman, Alison Kay, shocked by the recent death of a homeless man in the city. In the 40 years since its foundation, The People's Kitchen has provided friendship and food to anyone who needs it, serving more than 250 meals a day, 365 days a year, running entirely on voluntary effort and charitable donations. Looking at these two buildings sited just metres apart, but in other ways existing in two different universes, sparked for us the question: How does what goes on in there (the Catalyst) impact on the lives of the people in there (The People's Kitchen)?

The spark of serendipity that first lit the i3o flame was a meeting between Michael Glass from the University of Pittsburgh and Louise Kempton from Newcastle University (UK) in St Étienne in France at the end of 2018, at a conference for a project examining commonalities across older, deindustrialised regions. Louise was only attending to fill in for a colleague (former RSA President Mark Tewdwr-Jones, if memory serves!). Sharing details about their cities, they (Glass and Kempton) were immediately struck by the similarities in the economic histories of Pittsburgh and Newcastle: their population size, the prominent role of the "Eds and Meds" sectors, and a sense of peripherality in relation to bigger, better known cities. Thinking that there could be the basis for some interesting and relevant comparative work, a two-way exchange visits for spring 2020 were organised, thanks to the generous support of a Jean Monnet Network grant at the University of Pittsburgh (which had to be postponed until 2022 thanks to COVID-19).

At the time, Pittsburgh was about to execute plans for an innovation district, Hazelwood Green, based on the site of a former steel mill and adjacent to the neighbourhood of Hazelwood, which had suffered from extreme depopulation and other economic challenges over decades. We had found the hook for a Newcastle–Pittsburgh comparative study.

i3o BEGINS

With some internal funding support from Newcastle University, we started to work on a pilot study of the Helix, to develop and test a methodology that we could later apply in Pittsburgh. At this point David Marlow joined the emergent team. With a wealth of experience as a former senior policy leader, now working as an independent consultant and Visiting Professor of Practice in Louise's research centre,[1] David was the ideal person to help turn our ideas into action.

With the Newcastle study complete, we went back to Pittsburgh to work on the comparative study, adding Sabina Detrick to the team. We felt we were onto something; the approach seemed to work, and we were finding out interesting opportunities and differences from our international comparative approach. Local actors were engaged with and enthusiastic about what we were doing, and there was an appetite to share the learning between the two cities.

With the first two case studies focused on inclusive innovation in two post-industrial cities in the Global North finding so much in common, we were keen to add a "Global South" case to the mix. Medellín in Colombia came instantly to mind, having been named the World's Most Innovative City by the *Wall Street Journal* in 2013, amongst many other accolades.[2] As it happened (in another piece of serendipity), Louise had just been invited to join a panel at a conference there at the end of 2023, and David had a connection to the head of their innovation district. It looked like Medellín was shaping up to be our next case study.

THE TEAM EXPANDS

With Medellín now in scope to be the third i3o case study, David, Michael and Louise attended the Annual RSA 2023 Conference in Ljubljana, Slovenia, where we shared our preliminary findings from the Newcastle and Pittsburgh case studies. During the opening reception we bumped into Diana Morales and Luke Green. Diana was an early-career researcher based in Sweden with a strong background in innovation and regional development studies who had completed her doctorate at Newcastle's Centre of Urban and Regional Development Studies (CURDS). Luke was a doctoral student, also at CURDS, researching university investments in real estate, which brought another valuable set of skills and knowledge to the team. The fact that Diana is also a Colombian citizen made the case for exploring a Medellín case study even more compelling.

But we needed a good partner on the ground. The studies in Newcastle and Pittsburgh had reinforced the fact that including locally based researchers who know the landscape and have the right connections are essential to ensuring the process goes further than a superficial "windshield tour" that did not engage with the key players in the city. The RSA member database was invaluable. We knew we were likely to find someone like-minded within that network, and in Carlos Cadena from Universidad EAFIT in Medellín we were not disappointed!

Despite Medellín being a much bigger city than Newcastle and Pittsburgh, it turned out that the networks were tight. Either that or Carlos knows everyone you need to know in the city, also a likely scenario. Following an initial visit in December 2023, Diana, David and Luke successfully applied for an RSA Policy Expo grant that funded a research visit in May 2024, another important milestone in which the RSA played a critical role.

THE FOURTH PIECE OF THE JIGSAW

As we now had a "pair" in Newcastle and Pittsburgh (post-industrial cities reinventing themselves through research-led innovation), we needed to find a comparative case for Medellín. It happened the 25th anniversary of the Belfast Good Friday Agreement had just occurred and we reflected on the parallels with Medellín, where the end of the cartel wars had happened 30 years previously. Both places were now repositioning themselves as places of historical conflict into cities defined by innovation-led development.

In yet another example of academic serendipity, it transpired that Michael already had a longstanding collaboration with colleagues in geography and planning at Queen's University Belfast. And so, the fourth case study was locked down, with a scoping visit in March 2024 followed by a research visit in September the same year.

WHERE WE ARE NOW, AND WHERE TO NEXT

With Gareth Robinson from Queen's University the newest member of the team, i3o now comprises a significant international team based on three continents. But the i3o "family" is much greater, including policymakers, community representatives, and other actors across the four cities and beyond.

Thanks to an award from Newcastle University's Economic and Social Research Council (ESRC) Impact Acceleration Account (IAA) matched with IAA funds from Queen's University, we are (as of autumn 2025) in the process of returning to each city, taking policymakers and community members with us to foster peer-to-peer knowledge exchange. It has been humbling to witness the power of these new dialogues, which go far beyond what can be achieved through academic endeavour alone.

Our goal is to expand the i3o network to more UK and US post-industrial cities, other contexts such as rural economies, globally recognised exemplars from which we can learn rather than seek to emulate (always a path to failure) and, most importantly, more case studies from the so-called Global South, which, in our experience, we in the so-called North have much to learn from, something this book makes clear. We are keen to hear from others who are interested in joining the network if, after reading this book, you feel like your city's innovation ecosystem could benefit from enhancing its inclusive innovation journey.

THE IMPORTANCE OF (MANAGED) SERENDIPITY

Our final reflections on this journey to date is the importance of embracing serendipity and, to some extent, allowing the process to happen rather than trying to manage it. But being forced to articulate our story so far has made us realise three things: the role of learned societies such as the RSA is vital in finding your tribe – conferences and other events are critical moments to forge new connections and cement existing ones; even a modest amount of institutional support (such as we have had from Newcastle University, the University of Pittsburgh and Queen's University Belfast) can be pivotal in keeping the train on the tracks; and never underestimate the impact a casual conversation over a coffee or a beer might have. New technology is incredibly valuable in keeping existing connections alive, but will never replace the in-person interactions that are essential to establishing important cross-boundary policy projects.

NOTES

1 CURDS (Centre of Urban and Regional Development Studies).

2 https://cities-today.com/medellin-takes-top-urban-innovation-award/

Michael R. Glass, Louise Kempton, David Marlow, Luke Green,
Carlos Cadena-Gaitán, Sabina Deitrick and Diana Morales
The i3o team, January 2026

Executive summary and actionable insights

This book describes the Improving Inclusive Innovation Outcomes (i3o) research programme (2022–25). This work recognises that place-based economic growth in the 21st century is called to deliver more equitable and sustainable outcomes that address social challenges. The i3o programme focuses on inclusive innovation in urban innovation districts: geographical concentrations of assets and amenities designed to deliver economic growth for their host cities. i3o engaged with four cities in post-industrial (Newcastle, Pittsburgh) and post-conflict (Medellín, Belfast) cities. Each city's innovation district express commitments to inclusive growth and is shifting towards a new model – what we define here as Innovation Districts 2.0. This emerging model repositions innovation policy around purposeful leadership, community engagement and place-based strategic alignment. We argue that these cities reflect steps toward a new best-practice model that other existing and potential innovation districts can learn from and integrate in their own cities.

Chapter 2 synthesises the evolution of academic thinking on inclusive innovation. Chapter 3 proposes a methodology and toolkit for helping places define inclusive innovation in ways that reflect their local context and culture and diagnose how their innovation district creates effective outcomes for communities and local businesses. Chapter 4 explains the innovation journey of each city and their innovation ecosystems. Chapter 5 provides the findings of the i3o analysis in each city. We find the toolkit has considerable validity to assess inclusive innovation across urban contexts. Chapter 6 concludes by suggesting the relevance of this work for places interested in inclusive innovation. It proposes steps that these and other cities can choose to follow to capture the promise of an Innovation District 2.0 model of inclusion-rich development.

An Innovation District 2.0 will be characterised by purposeful inclusive innovation: leadership and management; by proactive community engagement and placemaking; and by strategic alignment and territorial equity awareness of their contributions to relevant city growth strategies.

https://doi.org/10.1080/2578711X.2025.2624330

Innovation District 2.0 leadership and management will embrace:

(1) *Purposefulness*: in discussing, agreeing, and publicising an explicit inclusive innovation vision and priorities that they will be committed to progressing.
(2) *Business planning*: ensuring business planning and performance management systems are fit for purpose for delivering those inclusive innovation goals.
(3) *Curation*: calibrating the mix of tenants, activities and networks within the innovation district to foster and strengthen inclusive innovation policy and practice.
(4) *Community agency*: to arrive at a consensus with relevant communities of place and interest about how they should be engaged in planning and managing the district.

In terms of community engagement and placemaking, an Innovation District 2.0:

(1) Enables *inclusive, accessible placemaking*: codesigning welcoming spaces, transport and housing that are accessible to local communities and the wider city.
(2) Addresses *relevant societal challenges*: encouraging projects and programmes that improve experiences and opportunities for local communities and businesses.
(3) Delivers *short-term wins* that build local confidence in, and a commitment to, the generational vision and profound changes a successful district will create.
(4) Balances *perspectives and priorities* of adjacent communities with the voices and needs of disadvantaged communities in the wider city region.

The strategic alignment and territorial equity positioning of an Innovation District 2.0:

(1) Identifies, agrees and makes *distinct measurable contributions to city-inclusive growth* and other relevant strategies.
(2) *Has territorial equity awareness* of spatial, economic and social impacts on the development pathways of towns and communities more distant from the innovation district.

All three characteristics of the framework will deliver inclusion-rich local strengths that enable Innovation Districts 2.0 to look beyond copying orthodox global best practice to be the best innovation district they can be for their city-region.

As a Regional Studies Association (RSA) Policy Impact book, we intend for it to be accessible and actionable for all members of urban innovation ecosystems, whether from the community, government, academia or industry. This book sets out what we intend to be a broader research agenda to assist innovation districts deliver broader social outcomes. Based on our first four case studies, we propose three insights:

- Place-leaders can define "inclusive innovation" and use their definition for existing or planned innovation districts and equivalents. The i3o method, toolkit and Innovation District 2.0 characteristics are a starting point. They can be tailored and adapted locally.

- i3o demonstrates replicable and scalable academic–policy exchange for this and other grand place-based challenges. It brought together local universities, policymakers, and community-role players to deliberate and develop inclusive innovation actionable insights. The four cities are all enthusiastic about an enduring community of practice. This will facilitate continued learning in and across places.
- The Innovation District 2.0 concept promises a viable, ambitious model we believe can be adapted to deliver improving inclusive innovation outcomes in any place.

Innovation has always been in the forefront of delivering change; this book seeks to ensure that all places have the methods and tools available to deliver that change inclusively and successfully.

1. Improving inclusive innovation outcomes for innovation districts

1.1 WHY DOES INCLUSIVE INNOVATION MATTER FOR CITIES?

The crux of innovation is producing something new or different to the world, and it represents a seductive goal for firms, cities and regions that feel their competitive edge becoming dulled. If a city-region has undergone traumatic change, for example, from enjoying decades of manufacturing-based economic growth and employment opportunities to facing an uncertain "post-industrial" future, or a region whose capacity to attract residents and inward investment has suffered from decades of structural violence, then the idea of introducing something new or different is likely to be enticing from a policy perspective. This Policy Impact book deals with the consequences of four cities that are using innovation-based strategies to address a multifaceted and complex set of challenges related to broader economic (and, in some cases, political) restructuring. In each of these cities, science, technology and research-led innovation (STRI) represents an increasingly important approach by local economic development strategists and policymakers for envisioning and achieving more prosperous futures for their urban and regional economies. Each of these cities wants to create economic development strategies focused on innovation ecosystems and innovation districts, as the cities look to recover from the loss of their historic economic engines. These four cases thus represent part of a broader global movement of cities and regions that are seeking to renew themselves by bringing together new strategies and resources to enhance urban innovation districts.

While there is nothing inherently bad about innovation-led growth as a policy target, policymakers are increasingly becoming aware of the potential problems that mainstream approaches can cause.[1] Research from regional studies confirms that, left unchecked, innovation policies can cause increasing social and economic inequality and change neighbourhoods in ways that disadvantage the residents who are expected to welcome the arrival of new investments.[2] These are valid concerns, as are complaints that innovation districts (often featuring high-quality placemaking and located in the shadow of prestigious universities) do little for local businesses not linked to innovation district supply chains, or for the job prospects of nearby residents, and particularly those who are less economically secure. However, there are ways to avoid these problems, and to unleash the potential of innovation in ways that maximise public benefits. This involves creating policies that address these challenges directly, and that make sure that the "success" of STRI is defined beyond standard measures of economic growth or business scale-ups to incorporate broader societal goals such as local workforce opportunities and educational attainment. The phrase "inclusive innovation" is now gaining traction as a concept that responds to the limited benefits that traditional innovation investments can create for local communities.[3]

This Policy Impact book demonstrates how inclusive innovation can support more equitable and sustainable forms of urban transformation, drawing on the real-world example of four innovation districts. As places where collaboration between university, business,

https://doi.org/10.1080/2578711X.2026.2624322

community and government happens (the so-called "quadruple helix"),[4] often in locations needing physical regeneration and reinvestment, innovation districts serve as important physical locations for developing and delivering inclusive innovation strategies. Through comparative case study analysis and qualitative research in Belfast (UK), Newcastle upon Tyne (UK), Medellín (Colombia) and Pittsburgh (USA) we provide insights that policymakers, civic leaders and community stakeholders can use in their own cities to achieve more impactful forms of innovation through designing and developing innovation districts that foster and support inclusion.

The book describes three specific and original contributions from the Improving Inclusive Innovation Outcomes (i3o) project: a three-year collaboration between researchers and policy partners to understand approaches to delivering inclusive innovation. As we outline in the preface, this collaboration arose serendipitously through institutional connections between Newcastle University and the University of Pittsburgh, and the awareness that Pittsburgh and Newcastle (as well as Medellín and Belfast) were all facing similar processes of innovation-led reinvention and significant social and economic disparities between the districts and their neighbouring communities. This book represents the first steps toward a fuller international research agenda that intends to assist the participants of local innovation ecosystems in developing broader impacts from the generational investments that innovation districts represent.

We hold that inclusive innovation need not be a vague or "fuzzy" concept.[5] Instead, we suggest that regions can gain a lot from actively pursuing inclusive innovation, but that this means building a tailored strategic approach to deliver meaningful results to local communities, stakeholders and supply chains. Quality placemaking alone is a necessary but insufficient element for delivering inclusive innovation. Our research in post-industrial and post-conflict cities finds three things need to occur:

- Inclusive innovation strategies need to be championed by purposeful leadership and management.
- Inclusion needs meaningful engagement and collaboration with communities before innovation district planning has even begun.
- Innovation districts need to be aligned strategically with local economic and social development priorities.

1.2 INCLUSIVE INNOVATION: THE NEED FOR INNOVATION DISTRICTS 2.0

Urban innovation districts are an increasingly popular tool used by city leaders since the 2000s to drive economic development and mark a shift of innovation sites back to city centres from suburban science parks, the dominant spatial model of the latter 20th century. Universities are becoming increasingly prominent in developing these spaces which typically bring together research institutions, businesses and entrepreneurs.[6] These urban innovation districts are areas where businesses, supporting organisations and public agencies are encouraged to locate together to stimulate innovation.[7] Innovation districts are designed as mixed-use environments in central urban locations where there is easy access to research universities, government agencies and transportation. These districts often appear distinct from their surrounding communities through master planning that includes attractive housing options, high-quality public spaces, adaptive reuse of existing buildings and other supportive infrastructure (see Box 1.1). The considerable cost associated with creating innovation districts is justified by promises of collaboration, inward investment, urban regeneration and, ultimately, regional economic growth.[8] Innovation districts are now a common sight in cities across the globe, but they have proved particularly attractive to policymakers in cities seeking to overcome historic challenges by defining new economic development futures.

However, the tendency of innovation districts to distinguish themselves from their surrounding communities (both physically and in terms of economic activities), and the emphasis on economic growth goals, can lead to exclusionary outcomes. Such outcomes can occur if the innovation districts reinforce a division between central cities and the region in general, and a growing division within cities due to the success of these districts can have negative impacts for long-time nearby residents as housing prices threaten displacement or otherwise exclude long-term residents while not creating outcomes that meet local needs or benefit local communities.[9]

Box 1.1 Adaptive reuse of Mill 19, Hazelwood Green

The Hazelwood Green innovation district is under construction on the site of the former Jones & Laughlin Steel Company mill and coke works in Pittsburgh, Pennsylvania. Most of the industrial heritage of this 178-acre site was demolished and cleared, but Mill 19 was retained and redeveloped into an advanced manufacturing research centre in the heart of the new district. The mill's superstructure was retained and substantially modified to provide flexible incubator space for firms. The building features the largest rooftop solar array in the United States (generating enough energy to power 380 homes), sustainable urban drainage systems and a public plaza for events. The structure is adjacent to the University of Pittsburgh's bioengineering centre (BioForge), and Carnegie Mellon University's Robotics Innovation Center.

The key policy challenge is overcoming innovation district models that unintentionally reinforce socio-economic disparities, concentrating benefits among elite institutions and high-skilled workers, while marginalised communities remain excluded from decision-making and

Figure 1.1 Innovation district placemaking in Pittsburgh's Hazelwood Green.

Photo: Louise Kempton, September 2025.

opportunities for development. Broader challenges await if cities do not extend innovation benefits to their surrounding regions; regional inclusion would mean that regional innovation ecosystems are supported and linked to the benefits created by cities and their innovation districts.[10] Solving these problems and unleashing the power of innovation districts to address wider challenges will require designing innovation districts that can catalyse economic growth and change for a wider set of communities, supply chains and organisations. This goal is summarised as "inclusive innovation" – an increasingly popular concept for researchers, policymakers and community advocates.

Inclusive innovation is a hotly debated term because what "inclusion" looks like can vary from group to group and from place to place. In this book, inclusive innovation is defined as the "co-creation of new ideas, practices or technologies with local communities, businesses and organisations to address societal challenges, ensuring equitable benefit distribution and fostering community empowerment".[11] Innovation districts matter for inclusive innovation precisely because they are key arenas where innovation solutions to these societal challenges can be developed.

This book showcases the inclusive potential of innovation districts through four cities that have embraced innovation district strategies while also confronting distinct challenges:

Newcastle upon Tyne: a post-industrial city in North East England, Newcastle has invested in the Helix innovation district, a flagship site co-developed by Newcastle University, Newcastle City Council and Legal & General, one of the world's largest investment management firms. Despite its ambitions for sustainable urban living and community connectivity, Helix sits adjacent to some of the city's most deprived neighbourhoods, raising questions about benefit distribution and community agency.

Pittsburgh: once a steel manufacturing powerhouse, Pittsburgh's Hazelwood Green innovation district is a philanthropic foundation-led redevelopment of a former mill and coke works site. Anchored by major university investments, but set a few kilometres from the university precinct of Oakland and the more established Pittsburgh innovation district, Hazelwood Green aspires to deliver inclusive economic opportunity. Yet its governance structure and physical location pose challenges for transparency, accountability and community engagement.

Medellín: a city that has transformed its global image from one of violence to innovation, Medellín's Ruta N (now FutuMED) innovation district exemplifies inclusive innovation through social urbanism. Located in a historically marginalised area, the district integrates public infrastructure, education and participatory planning. Medellín's experience offers a viable alternative to STRI strategies that focus on knowledge and technology.

Belfast: emerging from decades of sectarian conflict, Belfast is developing a dispersed innovation ecosystem supported by the Belfast Region City Deal. While the city's innovation strategy emphasises employability and digital skills, broader inclusion goals – such as supporting the foundational economy and long-term community engagement – remain underdeveloped.

This Policy Impact book offers a guide to policymakers interested in cutting-edge innovation district strategies that can create a wider set of outcomes than early adopters of the innovation district approach managed to achieve. Drawing on grounded research and comparative analysis, it offers a framework for unleashing the potential of inclusive innovation in cities undergoing profound transformation, what we are referring to in this book as "Innovation Districts 2.0".

1.3 THE BOOK'S STRUCTURE

Taken together, the chapters guide readers through the conceptual, methodological, and practical dimensions to design and deliver inclusive innovation. Chapter 2 introduces the concept of inclusive innovation, placing the idea within a rapidly evolving set of research literatures and debates on innovation. It highlights how innovation districts are more influenced by regional (rather than national) governance, tracks the rise of mission-oriented approaches and traces the emergence of inclusive innovation as a response to social challenges.

Chapter 3 outlines the research methodology. The i3o research involved repeat site visits, expert interviews, policy roundtables and community outreach. The project also created a practical "toolkit" with which to diagnose challenges and develop targeted recommendations for city leaders interested in pursuing inclusive innovation. The chapter explains this toolkit, and how it can be applied by readers in their own contexts.

Chapter 4 introduces the case studies. We explain how the cities were selected and explain the profound research and policy benefits that arise when conducting comparative global research. We then describe the four cases through three different phases of their (ongoing) development. We examine the *triggers* for innovation district formation, looking at the leadership structures, historic development and current problems that each city faced. We then describe the *evolution* phase for the innovation districts, examining how the place-based leadership coalitions in each city sought to use inclusion as part of a new innovation district strategy. We end the chapter by evaluating the current state of the innovation districts in each city: the "Towards Innovation District 2.0" phase. The four cities are at different stages of their district formation strategies, providing readers a chance to relate these cases to their own local conditions.

Chapter 5 brings together lessons and learnings from the case studies. We place inclusive innovation at the centre of our findings and show how three elements are crucial for making sure that innovation districts can lean into their potential as transformative sites in urban locations. First, we explain the importance of purposeful leadership and transparent governance to an inclusive innovation journey. Second, we highlight the need for sincere community engaged processes. Third, we stress that inclusive innovation strategies must align with city-region priorities. We argue that all three of these elements are equally important and mutually dependent; policymakers cannot adopt a "pick-and-mix" approach to the design of inclusive innovation strategies.

Chapter 6 provides policy recommendations for city and community leaders, planners, and institutional representatives as a series of actionable insights. We advocate for embedding inclusive innovation into urban planning, aligning innovation district investments with social value goals and call for greater cross-sector collaboration. The research findings from our four cases makes clear that an "Innovation District 2.0" model is achievable for all districts regardless of their maturity: leadership, engagement and alignment hold the key to inclusive innovation.

NOTES

1 Lee N (2023) Inclusive innovation in cities: from buzzword to policy. *Regional Studies*, 59(1): 2168637. https://doi.org/10.1080/00343404.2023.2168637

2 Clark J (2020) *Uneven Innovation: The Work of Smart Cities*. New York: Columbia University Press; Kayanan CM (2022) A critique of innovation districts: Entrepreneurial living and the burden of shouldering urban development. *Environment & Planning A* 54: 50–66; Wolf-Powers L (2022) *University City: History, Race, and Community in the Era of the Innovation District*. Philadelphia: University of Pennsylvania Press.

3 Morales D, Green L, Marlow D, Cadena Gaitán C, Deitrick S, Glass MR and Kempton L (2025) Defining inclusive innovation: Challenges and lessons for innovation districts. *Regional Studies, Regional Science*, 12(1): 740–753, https://doi.org/10.1080/21681376.2025.2543915

4 Vallance P, Tewdwr-Jones M, and Kempton L. (2020) Building collaborative platforms for urban innovation: Newcastle City Futures as a quadruple helix intermediary. *European Urban and Regional Studies*, 27(4): 325–341. https://doi.org/10.1177/0969776420905630

5 Lee (2023), see Reference 1.

6 Kempton L, Marlow D, Deitrick S, Glass M and Travis R (2024) Swimming against the tide: The role for social sciences and humanities in contributing to a more inclusive approach to innovation in post-industrial cities. In F Spigarelli, L Kempton and L Campagnucci (Eds.), *Entrepreneurship & Digital Humanities*. Cheltenham: Edward Elgar; Wolf-Powers (2022), see Reference 2.

7 Drucker J and Kayanan CM (2024) Innovation districts: Assessing their potential as a strategy for urban economic development. *Urban Affairs Review*, 60(3): 802–834.

8 Katz B and Wagner J (2014) *The Rise of Innovation Districts: A New Geography of Innovation in America*. Washington, DC: Brookings Institution.

9 Clark (2020), see Reference 2; Kayanan (2022), see Reference 2.

10 Kemeny T and Storper M (2020) *Superstar Cities and Left-Behind Places: Disruptive Innovation, Labor Demand, and Interregional Inequality* (Working Paper No. 41, February). London School of Economics (LSE).

11 Morales et al. (2025), p. 40, see Reference 3.

2. What are inclusive innovation districts? The conceptual and policy foundations

2.1 WHAT IS INNOVATION?

Innovation, as defined by the Organisation for Economic Co-operation and Development's (OECD) *Oslo Manual*, is "a new or improved product or process (or combination thereof) that differs significantly from the unit's previous products or processes and that has been made available to potential users (product) or brought into use by the unit (process)".[1] This definition highlights three essential elements. First, innovation is not merely about invention: it needs to go from the planning stage to generate actual value for a business. Second, innovation includes a wide range of activities beyond product development, such as organisational and process changes. Third, it is rooted in the context of private enterprise, focusing on activities that contribute to economic value.[2]

Innovation is a traditional driver of economic development. It is often presumed to be inherently positive, bringing inevitable benefits for individuals, communities and society. Yet a closer examination reveals that innovation is far from neutral. It can be divisive, extractive and deeply political.[3] Indeed, research and policy are increasingly calling the attention on innovation's uneven impacts, prompting shifts toward innovation policies that address societal challenges and promote inclusive growth in cities and regions.[4] These new ideas are leading to diverse, yet interrelated, approaches to innovation, and to a rethinking of innovation as both an academic and a policy concept.

Perspectives about the drivers of innovation have shifted over time. Innovation is no longer viewed solely as scientific or technological advancement driven by isolated researchers or inventors and is now seen as a systemic process involving a complex interplay of actors, institutions and sectors that policy can influence.[5] Geography also matters for innovation: the location and characteristics of place, such as infrastructure, networks, governance and socio-economic conditions, are essential for innovation to emerge, take root and scale.[6] Thus, while the term "innovation" refers broadly to introducing new or significantly improved products, processes or business methods that generate value, innovation policy is concerned with the frameworks, strategies and interventions that are intended to foster, guide and regulate these innovation activities.

Therefore, while innovation can significantly impact places, firms and sectors, enhancing job creation, competitiveness and long-term economic resilience, it can also increase inequality by concentrating its benefits in privileged groups and already competitive regions.[7] This leads us to ask: Must innovation be exclusive? How can we define and implement more inclusive approaches to innovation? These questions are at the heart of this Policy Impact book. This chapter lays the groundwork by exploring the concept of inclusive innovation. We first trace the evolution of innovation policy, assess its relevance in shaping inclusive outcomes and critically examine the role of innovation districts that frequently contribute to geographical inequalities, even as they are promoted as vehicles for inclusive innovation.[8]

https://doi.org/10.1080/2578711X.2026.2624324

2.2 THE EVOLUTION OF INNOVATION POLICY

Innovation policy has evolved significantly in three generations.[9] First, innovation for growth (traditional innovation policy) focused on funding basic research as part of national development priorities or to correct market failures to stimulate research and development (R&D) investment. Second, systems of innovation, which emphasise institutional and network dynamics for innovation. Third, transformative change, which reorients innovation toward addressing grand societal challenges through long-term, systemic transitions. Each approach reflects different rationales for policy intervention and implies distinct strategies and instruments. Inclusive innovation, it could be argued, occupies a space between second- and third-generation innovation policy. It aligns with second-generation approaches through its focus on institutional and network dynamics that promote growth and competitiveness. At the same time, it reflects third-generation concerns by addressing grand societal challenges, particularly those related to spatial and social inequality.

Innovation policy has emerged and evolved from a traditional emphasis on science and technology as the primary drivers for economic growth, and a recent sense that innovation is a tool that can solve societal challenges.[10] Modern innovation policy begins from the understanding that innovation involves the interplay of various actors and institutions that the public sector can influence.[11] This led to the development of national innovation systems (NIS) in the latter 20th century, and to innovation policies promoting networks of organisations in the public and private sectors whose activities and interactions initiate, modify and diffuse new technologies, including R&D departments, technological institutes and universities.[12]

A shift occurred when it was realised that local and regional contexts influence the emergence and diffusion of innovation, and that significant disparities in innovation outcomes were apparent across regions within the same country. The concept of regional innovation systems (RIS) emerged to counteract the national focus of innovation policy and NIS. RIS are networks of businesses, universities and other organisations in a specific area that work together, share knowledge and support each other to create new ideas, products or services.[13] This emphasis on regional outcomes occurred at a time when regions were gaining prominence as a key geographical scale to explain and promote innovation and economic growth.[14]

Innovation policy's third generation began in the 21st century by incorporating a purpose-driven approach due to the need to respond to contemporary existential societal challenges such as an ageing population, the climate emergency, mass migration, rapid technological change and the impacts of globalisation. This policy innovation in innovation policy reflects a growing recognition that successful innovation should drive economic growth while addressing societal goals including inclusivity and sustainability. Mission-oriented innovation policy focuses its efforts on promoting innovation that addresses societal challenges, by mobilising

Box 2.1 What makes for effective inclusive innovation?

Types of outcomes: innovation infrastructure and services must be designed to tackle local or regional challenges directly affecting communities, with STRI activities prioritising relevant solutions.

Distribution of benefits: initiatives must ensure that local communities and businesses receive tangible benefits from innovation district investments, including, but not limited to, opportunities for employment, training and access to essential resources for disadvantaged groups.

Community agency: inclusive innovation policies should actively involve local and marginalised communities in the process of design and implementation of the innovation districts, allowing a co-creation of strategies and priorities.

and coordinating public and private efforts under a defined mission as outlined by Mariana Mazzucato.[15]

Promoting inclusive innovation through innovation policy implies that interventions and investments in innovation and science, technology, and research-led innovation (STRI) are encouraged by local stakeholders following a framework that guides how governments and institutions invest in and coordinate efforts to support regional development and inclusive growth.[16] Accordingly, governments should focus on building research capacity and infrastructure, supporting technological development, encouraging innovation ecosystems, and aligning science and innovation with social and economic priorities. Effective inclusive innovation strategies should address the core elements outlined in Box 2.1.

Inclusive innovation is gaining traction within innovation policy, but tools and strategies are needed to help translate principles into practice. This is increasingly important as innovation districts become more popular as tools of local and regional economic development.[17] These geographically concentrated hubs, often located in urban areas that have suffered from historic disinvestment and deindustrialisation, are designed to distil the NIS and RIS goals of collaboration, entrepreneurship and technological advancement in urban centres linked to research universities and hubs of skilled capital. The idea of embedding innovation in urban areas with challenging development histories is often expected to lead organically to inclusive innovation outcomes, yet in practice requires a lot of intentional intervention to turn promises into reality.

2.3 INCLUSIVE INNOVATION

A growing consensus among researchers finds that innovation is not inherently beneficial for everyone or every place. Critics argue that investments in innovation, mostly in the form of STRI, tend to disproportionately benefit already privileged segments of society while producing uneven outcomes between and within cities and regions, reinforcing existing socio-economic divides.[18] Inequalities across individuals, communities and regions are increasingly recognised as significant consequences of innovation that demand policy attention.[19] Studies show that innovation plays a key role in shaping spatial economic inequality, concerns that are amplified as disruptive technologies such as artificial intelligence, robotics and decarbonisation technologies emerge.[20] Leaving these concerns unattended risks shaping *exclusive* innovation, where innovation activities privilege a limited set of groups and sectors, dampening the capacity of innovation to create broader economic and social benefits.[21]

The focus of innovation policies has shifted over time as these challenges have become clear.[22] The concept of inclusive innovation is a policy response to concerns about the distribution of innovation's benefits[23] and seeks benefits that are more widely distributed across society. However, defining inclusive innovation is complex. Inclusive innovation is distinct from social innovation. Although both share a focus on inclusion and addressing societal needs, social innovation emphasises creating inclusive relationships, particularly with groups historically excluded from mainstream economic, political or social processes. It also prioritises social impact over profit, and is often aimed at targeted domains such as education, health or migration.[24] While inclusive innovation intersects with social innovation, especially in its goals of equity and access, it continues to be tied to the broader innovation system and economic development strategies.

Supranational institutions such as the OECD emphasise the accessibility and participation of low-income groups in innovation activities to promote inclusive growth.[25] Inclusive innovation research is also highlighting how the innovation process can create new goods and services for low-income populations.[26] Other fields such as development studies have focused on the promotion of innovation activities in low-income countries,[27] while geographical research criticises the uneven distribution of innovation between and within regions.[28]

Delivering inclusive innovation means identifying the key factors that promote inclusiveness. Current research highlights elements such as education, entrepreneurship and stable employment as critical factors.[29] This mix can vary, with variations in local institutional capacity mattering in shaping what inclusive innovation policy should target. As a result, leaving inclusiveness as undefined can be strategically useful since it will depend on what local challenges exist and how the benefits of innovation should be distributed.

Accordingly, current research is trying to specify what inclusive innovation means in practice. Inclusive innovation goes beyond expanding access to new technologies or economic opportunities; it can also mean enhancing the quality and dignity of work for all workers, breaking down structural and institutional barriers to public participation in innovation activities, and building the capacity of peripheral or marginalised groups to benefit from innovation processes.[30]

We draw on these emerging strands of debate around the benefits of inclusion-rich innovation to construct a definition that can be used across different geographical contexts. We define inclusive innovation as:

> the co-creation of new ideas, practices, or technologies with local communities, businesses, and organisations to address societal challenges, ensuring equitable benefit distribution and fostering community empowerment.[31]

Inclusive innovation is shaped by place, and what is considered inclusive, and which areas or groups should be prioritised varies depending on local contexts and challenges. We propose seven dimensions that can serve as guiding categories for inclusive innovation (Figure 2.1).

The research interest in inclusive innovation is rooted in the real implications it has for policy action. Innovation policy plays a central role in determining who participates in innovation processes, who benefits from their outcomes, and how resources and opportunities are distributed across regions and populations. Exclusionary innovation can dampen the impact of public investments in the infrastructures of innovation, diminishing the prospects of innovation-based economic development strategies. Therefore, embedding inclusion goals into innovation policy is essential for ensuring that public investments in innovation are maximised, so that innovation contributes to broader societal well-being rather than reinforcing existing inequalities.

2.4 INCLUSIVE INNOVATION IN INNOVATION DISTRICTS

As cities increasingly invest in innovation districts to drive growth, the challenge lies in embedding social value and inclusion into these strategies. Innovation districts arose as a 21st-century solution to urban development problems. These physically delineated areas are designed to concentrate innovation activities and actors including enterprises and research institutions, often accompanied by high-amenity, mixed-use urban districts that can attract skilled workers and inward investment.[32] Innovation districts can now be found worldwide, following a similar formula to increase urban STRI outcomes, enhance economic growth, attract high skilled workers, provide employment opportunities for the local service-class workers and disadvantaged local populations, host multinational firms, and promote entrepreneurship.[33] However, research has shown that innovation districts can drive gentrification, and that housing in or near them can become unaffordable for service workers and residents in nearby communities. There are also highly uneven benefits that are concentrated among highly educated or skilled workers, and disconnections between the innovation district and the local businesses and communities that host them.[34]

Figure 2.1 Dimensions of inclusive innovation

Economic Inactivity

Address issues among individuals who are economically inactive, including people with disabilities, former convicts, and other economic barriers. Guarantee access to opportunities in the innovation economy.

Health and Wellbeing

Address issues of poor health outcomes, health inequalities and other barriers to healthy living prevalent in relevant local left-behind communities.

Gender Perspective

Ensure gender inclusivity in the urban and policy design, as well as for access STEM jobs.

Education

Promote education from preschool to college to equip individuals with skills needed to achieve high skilled careers.

Inclusive Integration

Integrate immigrants, youth, and other marginalized people into the workforce.

Poverty Alleviation and Social Cohesion

Tackle generational poverty and poverty traps, targeting at remedying senses of resentment and isolation as urban economies change.

Net Zero and Climate Adaptation

Co-create and develop decarbonisation solutions that are affordable and accessible to local communities and improve the resilience of households and neighbourhoods.

Innovation districts therefore present both opportunities and tensions for the pursuit of inclusive innovation. While they are often presented as drivers of economic growth and technological advancement, their success in delivering social value depends heavily on how they are designed and governed. Participation and community engagement are critical components in this process. Participation serves as a procedural tool to include relevant actors in decision-making,[35] while community engagement emphasises the autonomy and agency of local communities to influence the design, implementation and evaluation of innovation districts.

In innovation policy and STRI interventions, public participation is often assumed as part of the increasingly popular concept of the quadruple helix.[36] The quadruple helix expands the notion of traditional innovation systems (universities, governments and industry) to include civil society as key actors in the innovation ecosystem of a city or region. However, as with other untested elements of the contested quadruple helix concept,[37] more research is needed to test how public participation can overcome the inherent tensions when diverse types of partners are brought into a planning process. Non-institutionalised groups such as neighbourhood collectives, as well as individual citizens seen beyond their role as consumers, are also fundamental actors for public participation and, therefore, a key component of inclusive innovation.[38] The fundamental goal of public participation in innovation district development and operation is to avoid superficial engagement and to allow communities (including representation beyond the loudest voices) to co-construct place-based innovation interventions that are sensitive to community needs and aspirations.[39]

Participation and community engagement must be intentional and planned; it involves consultation but also shared decision-making and collective ownership of processes and outcomes. For innovation districts, community engagement requires participatory approaches that enable local and disadvantaged communities to have agency and influence in shaping the priorities and activities of the innovation district, as well as finding effective ways to interact, collaborate and be integrated within the innovation ecosystem. This might involve, for instance, use of public spaces or communal areas, including social capital infrastructure and services defined by local communities, to enhance collaborative opportunities.[40] To engage and deliver benefits to local communities and stakeholders, interactions must be multidirectional, with clear access points for communities. Relationships in the local context can drive different forms of engagement, but central is the presence of intermediaries or clear agents to help to deliver community outcomes.[41]

In Pittsburgh, for example, the local community has built ties through workforce training and development programmes, linked to new opportunities in the innovation district, and builds from its workforce and education objectives centred in its community plan. In Medellín, Ruta N created new social and economic opportunities with links in adjacent communities as part of the strategy of social urbanism, central in Medellín (Box 2.2). Have these been successful? Our cases point to significant tensions existing between economic development goals of

Box 2.2 The Ruta N innovation district in Medellín, Colombia: a hub for social urbanism

The city of Medellín has transitioned from a legacy of urban violence and industrial decline to create a new urban future based on innovation and entrepreneurship. Through institutional strengthening, private sector engagement and academic collaboration, the city managed to reduce violence and transform itself. These efforts laid the foundation for Medellín's evolution into a more prosperous and innovative city. Its transformation involved a decades-long process of different interventions, multi-actor collaborations, large investments in urban infrastructure, and a solid and long-term innovation strategy that prioritised social innovation, social urbanism (investment in urban infrastructure and connectivity focusing on marginalised communities), and science and technology.

Founded in 2009, the Ruta N innovation district became the flagship organisation for leading Medellín's innovation strategy by supporting businesses in knowledge-based sectors and fostering entrepreneurship.

Figure 2.2 The Ruta N innovation district in Medellín

Source: Ruta N

innovation districts and the distribution of benefits to nearby community and marginalised groups. To deliver community-identified opportunities and benefits from inclusive innovation sees the need to expand the innovation ecosystem to build social innovation strategies into the planning and development as early as possible in the innovation district, with clear communication lines and community input strategies, built with political support. As Chapter 3 notes, our tools and methodology for inclusive innovation do not depend on a point in time in the development, but on agency and dedication to an Improving Inclusive Innovation Outcomes (i3o) strategy from central stakeholders and built as early as possible into innovation district planning and development.

The success of innovation districts is also set by their governance and leadership structure. Governance is the key differentiator between thriving and stagnant districts and requires mission-driven entities to coordinate across sectors, facilitate partnerships and manage shared infrastructure. While innovation districts are often positioned as engines of equitable growth, their outcomes vary widely depending on how well leadership aligns district goals with broader urban strategies and community needs.[42] Research from the Brookings Institution further elaborates on the leadership dynamics within innovation districts, advocating for "anchor-plus" models where universities and hospitals collaborate with start-ups, civic organisations and local governments. Katz and Wagner argue that this approach fosters a more distributed leadership structure, enabling responsiveness to local contexts and enhancing innovation capacity.[43] Complementing this, the European Commission's Joint Research Centre links governance quality to measurable outcomes such as talent retention, start-up growth and spatial equity.[44] Across these studies, a clear consensus emerges: governance must be designed to support collaboration and inclusion; leadership should be visionary yet grounded in local realities; and management must be agile, data-informed and aligned with long-term urban development goals. Innovation districts are not merely spatial clusters: they are complex ecosystems requiring thoughtful stewardship to realise their transformative potential.

2.5 CONCLUSIONS

This chapter has laid the conceptual and policy foundations for understanding inclusive innovation as a systemic, context-sensitive and socially oriented approach to innovation. We began by emphasising that innovation is not inherently inclusive and often produces uneven outcomes between and within regions and populations. Inclusive innovation, therefore, requires deliberate policy interventions that prioritise equity, participation and place-based strategies. We clarified its distinction from social innovation, while identifying core elements such as improving the dignity of work, expanding participation and enabling marginalised geographies to benefit from innovation processes.

While innovation districts are a popular policy tool, there is both a positive and a negative side to how they function in practice. While they are often positioned as catalysts for inclusive growth, their impacts, such as gentrification and exclusion, reveal tensions between inclusive innovation goals and social outcomes. We argue that meaningful participation and community engagement, on the one hand, and visionary leadership and governance, on the other, are essential to bridging this gap.

Inclusive innovation must be embedded not only in policy rhetoric but also in the design, governance, and evaluation of innovation ecosystems and innovation districts. The aim of inclusive innovation is to craft more equitable innovation policies; thus, it requires intentionality in creating policies that better align with community needs and aspirations, ensuring that these communities are seen as passive recipients and also as co-creators of the policies and interventions. Innovation districts are centres for modern STRI with potential to become key arenas for promoting inclusive innovation, yet there are several challenges that policy must first address.

NOTES

1 OECD (2018) *Oslo Manual 2018: Guidelines for Collecting, Reporting and Using Data on Innovation, 4th Edition*, at 60. Organisation for Economic Co-operation and Development. https://www.oecd.org/content/dam/oecd/en/publications/reports/2018/10/oslo-manual-2018_g1g9373b/9789264304604-en.pdf

2 Marques P, Morgan K and Richardson R (2018) Social innovation in question: The theoretical and practical implications of a contested concept. *Environment and Planning C: Politics and Space*, 36(3): 496–512. https://doi.org/10.1177/2399654417717986

3 Schrock G and Lowe N (2021) Inclusive Innovation Editorial: The promise of inclusive innovation. *Local Economy: The Journal of the Local Economy Policy Unit*, 36(3): 181–186. https://doi.org/10.1177/02690942211042254

4 Boschma R, Fitjar RD, Giuliani E and Iammarino S (2025) Unseen costs: The inequities of the geography of innovation. *Regional Studies*, 59(1): 2445594 . https://doi.org/10.1080/00343404.2024.2445594; Lee N (2019) Inclusive growth in cities: A sympathetic critique. *Regional Studies*, 53(3): 424–434.

5 Binz C and Castaldi C (2024) Toward a normative turn in research on the geography of innovation? Evolving perspectives on innovation, institutions, and human well-being. *Progress in Economic Geography*, 2(2): 100018. https://doi.org/10.1016/j.peg.2024.100018; Fagerberg J and Sapprasert K (2011) National innovation systems: The emergence of a new approach. *Science and Public Policy*, 38(9): 669–679. https://doi.org/10.3152/030234211X13070021633369

6 Asheim BT and Gertler MS (2009) The geography of innovation: Regional innovation systems. In J Fagerberg and D. Mowery (eds.), *Oxford Handbook of Innovation* (pp. 1–31). Oxford University Press; Tödtling F and Trippl M (2018) Regional innovation policies for new path development – Beyond neo-liberal and traditional systemic views. *European Planning Studies*, 26(9): 1779–1795. https://doi.org/10.1080/09654313.2018.1457140

7 Kemeny T, Petralia S and Storper M (2025) Disruptive innovation and spatial inequality. *Regional Studies*, 59(1): 2076824. https://doi.org/10.1080/00343404.2022.2076824

8 Kayanan CM (2022) A critique of innovation districts: Entrepreneurial living and the burden of shouldering urban development. *Environment & Planning A*, 54(1): 50–66. https://doi.org/10.1177/0308518X21104944

9 Schot J and Steinmueller WE (2018) Three frames for innovation policy: R&D, systems of innovation and transformative change. *Research Policy*, 47(9): 1554–1567. https://doi.org/10.1016/j.respol.2018.08.011

10 Isaksen A, Tödtling F and Trippl M (2018) Innovation policies for regional structural change: Combining actor-based and system-based strategies. In A Isaksen, R Martin and M Trippl (Eds.), *New Avenues for Regional Innovation Systems – Theoretical Advances, Empirical Cases and Policy Lessons* (pp. 221–238). Cham: Springer. http://link.springer.com/10.1007/978-3-319-71661-9_11

11 Lundvall BÅ (2016) *The Learning Economy and the Economics of Hope*. Anthem. https://library.oapen.org/handle/20.500.12657/31613; Asheim BT, Isaksen A and Trippl M (2021) The role of the regional innovation system approach in contemporary regional policy: Is it still relevant in a globalised world? In M Gonzalez-Lopez and BT Asheim (Eds.), *Regions and Innovation and Innovation Policies in Europe: Learning from the Margins* (pp. 12–29). Cheltenham: Edward Elgar.

12 López-Rubio P, Roig-Tierno N and Mas-Verdú F (2022) Assessing the origins, evolution and prospects of national innovation systems. *Journal of the Knowledge Economy*, 13(1): 161–184. https://doi.org/10.1007/s13132-020-00712-7

13 Cooke P (1992) Regional innovation systems: Competitive regulation in the new Europe. *Geoforum*, 23(3): 365–182. https://doi.org/10.1016/0016-7185(92)90048-9

14 Storper M (1997) *Regional Worlds*. New York: Guilford.

15 Mazzucato M (2018) Mission-oriented innovation policies: Challenges and opportunities. *Industrial and Corporate Change*, 27(5): 803–815. https://doi.org/10.1093/icc/dty034

16 United Nations Conference on Trade and Development (UNCTAD) (2019). *Beyond Uncertainty. UNCTAD Annual Report*, 2019. https://unctad.org/annualreport/2019/Pages/index.html

17 Katz B and Wagner J (2014) *The Rise of Innovation Districts: A New Geography of Innovation in America*. Washington, DC: Brookings Institution.

18 Boschma et al. (2025), see Reference 4; Planes-Satorra S and Paunov C (2017) *Inclusive Innovation Policies: Lessons from International Case Studies* (OECD Science, Technology and Industry Working Papers). https://www.oecd-ilibrary.org/science-and-technology/inclusive-innovation-policies_a09a3a5d-en; Unger RM, Stanley I and Gabriel M (2019) *Imagination Unleashed. Democratising the Knowledge Economy*. https://media.nesta.org.uk/documents/Imagination_unleashed-_Democratising_the_knowledge_economy_v6.pdf

19 Planes-Satorra and Paunov (2017), see Reference 18.

20 Kemeny et al. (2025), see Reference 7.

21 Schrock and Lowe (2021), see Reference 3.

22 Coenen L and Morgan K (2020) Evolving geographies of innovation: Existing paradigms, critiques and possible alternatives. *Norsk Geografisk Tidsskrift – Norwegian Journal of Geography*, 74(1): 13–24 https://doi.org/10.1080/00291951.2019.1692065; Schot and Steinmueller (2018), see Reference 9.

23 Lee (2019), see Reference 4; Lee N (2023) Inclusive innovation in cities: From buzzword to policy. *Regional Studies*, 59(1): 2168637. https://doi.org/10.1080/00343404.2023.2168637

24 Marques et al. (2018), see Reference 2.

25 OECD (2015) *Innovation Policies for Inclusive Growth*. Paris: Organisation for Economic Co-operation and Development (OECD) Publ. https://doi.org/10.1787/9789264229488-en

26 Chataway J, Hanlin R and Kaplinsky R (2014) Inclusive innovation: An architecture for policy development. *Innovation and Development*, 4(1): 33–54. https://doi.org/10.1080/2157930X.2013.876800; Foster C and Heeks R (2013) Conceptualising inclusive innovation: Modifying systems of innovation frameworks to understand diffusion of new technology to low-income consumers. *European Journal of Development Research*, 25(3): 333–355. https://doi.org/10.1057/ejdr.2013.7

27 Pansera M and Owen R (2018) Framing inclusive innovation within the discourse of development: Insights from case studies in India. *Research Policy*, 4(71): 22–34. https://doi.org/10.1016/j.respol.2017.09.007

28 Iammarino S, Rodriguez-Pose A and Storper M (2019) Regional inequality in Europe: Evidence, theory and policy implications. *Journal of Economic Geography*, 19(2): 273–298. https://doi.org/10.1093/jeg/lby021; Kemeny T and Osman T (2018) The wider impacts of high-technology employment: Evidence from US cities. *Research Policy*, 47(9): 1729–1740. https://doi.org/10.1016/j.respol.2018.06.005

29 Dubb S, McKinley S and Howard T (2013) *Achieving the Anchor Promise: Improving Outcomes for Children, Families and Communities* (Tacoma Park: The Democracy Collaborative & Annie E. Casey Foundation).

30 Schrock and Lowe (2021), see Reference 3.

31 Morales D, Green L, Marlow D, Cadena Gaitán C, Deitrick S, Glass M, et al. (2025) Defining inclusive innovation: Challenges and lessons for innovation districts. *Regional Studies, Regional Science*, 12(1): 740–753. https://doi.org/10.1080/21681376.2025.2543915

32 Clark J, Huang HW and Walsh J (2010) A typology of "innovation districts": What it means for regional resilience. *Cambridge Journal of Regions, Economy, and Society*, 3(1): 121–137.

33 Kayanan (2022), see Reference 8.

34 Drucker J and Kayanan CM (2024) Innovation districts: Assessing their potential as a strategy for urban economic development. *Urban Affairs Review*, 60(3): 802–834. https://doi.org/10.1093/cjres/rsp034

35 Bobbio L (2019) Designing effective public participation. *Policy and Society*, 38(1): 41–57. https://doi.org/10.1080/14494035.2018.1511193

36 Schütz F, Heidingsfelder M and Schraudner M (2019) Co-shaping the future in quadruple helix innovation systems: Uncovering public preferences toward participatory research and innovation. *She Ji: The Journal of Design, Economics, & Innovation*, 5(2): 128–146. https://doi.org/10.1016/j.sheji.2019.04.002

37 Hakeem M, Goi HC, Frendy and Ito H (2023) Regional sustainable development using a quadruple helix approach in Japan. *Regional Studies, Regional Science*, 10(1): 119–138. https://doi.org/10.1080/21681376.2023.2171313

38 Hofer K and Kaufmann D (2023) Actors, arenas and aims: A conceptual framework for public participation. *Planning Theory*, 22(4): 357–379. https://doi.org/10.1177/1473095222113958

39 Morales et al. (2025), see Reference 31.

40 Tomaney J, Blackman M, Natarajan L, Panayotopoulos-Tsiros D, Sutcliffe-Braithwaite F and Taylor M (2023) *Social Infrastructure and Left-Behind Places*. London: Routledge.

41 Bramwell A (2021) Inclusive innovation and the "ordinary" city: Incidental or integral? *Local Economy: The Journal of the Local Economy Policy Unit*, 36(3): 242–264. https://doi.org/10.1177/02690942211019005

42 Uyarra E (2010) Conceptualizing the regional roles of universities, implications and considerations. *European Planning Studies*, 18(8): 1227–1246. https://doi.org/10.1080/09654311003791275

43 Katz and Wagner (2014), see Reference 17.

44 Gianelle C, Guzzo F, Barbero Jimenez J and Salotti S (2024) The governance of regional innovation policy and its economic implications. *Annals of Regional Science*, 72(4): 1231–1254. https://doi.org/10.1007/s00168-023-01241-2

3. A methodology for diagnosing inclusion in innovation districts: the i3o toolkit

3.1 INTRODUCTION

The case for addressing inclusive innovation in contemporary inclusive growth policy and practice, and for science, technology and research-led innovation (STRI) programmes such as innovation districts, in particular, has risen up the policy agenda for reasons outlined in Chapter 2. We proposed a place-based definition for inclusive innovation with three distinctive dimensions: measurable societal outcomes, broad distribution of benefits, and meaningful community agency and involvement. In this chapter, we explain how inclusive innovation might be diagnosed, tested and developed to assist in making the definition "real" in specific contexts.

3.2 PRINCIPLES FOR IMPROVING INCLUSIVE INNOVATION OUTCOMES

The Improving Inclusive Innovation Outcomes (i3o) programme has deployed a process consultation approach[1] to diagnose where an innovation district, city or wider city-region is on its journey toward becoming an "Innovation District 2.0" which prioritises inclusive innovation. The key markers of a district on this journey include explicit acknowledgement that inclusion is a policy priority, defined priorities that intend to deliver an inclusion-rich innovation district and intervention strategies to ensure inclusion goals are maintained. These principles underpin the i3o approach and are shown in Figure 3.1.

Making inclusive innovation part of an innovation district's DNA means leadership teams and partner organisations need to agree upon a locally relevant definition for what inclusion

Figure 3.1 Principles for collaborative inclusive innovation research and policy development

Principle 1	Create an inclusive coalition of the willing
Principle 2	Be deliberative and developmental—not evaluative
Principle 3	Provide independent, informed and critical facilitation
Principle 4	Develop long term relationships and communities of practice
Principle 5	Build an adaptable methodology and toolkit

https://doi.org/10.1080/2578711X.2026.2624325

means for their district. This is an archetypal "wicked problem"[2] best addressed through process consultation approaches.

This type of collaborative, action research requires building trust with participating innovation districts, and this needs four ingredients: (1) a willing "client" or beneficiaries; (2) a methodological approach that is deliberative rather than judgemental; (3) openness to having independent, informed facilitators that lead a structured, inclusive and deliberative process; and (4) having an upfront intention to build a long-term relationship beyond the formal case study.

Adaptive leadership approaches focus on mobilising local role-players to conduct the difficult work of diagnosing and responding to the inclusive innovation challenges themselves. This is preferable to either seeking a quick fix or getting involved in win–lose judgements of activity and results that are often going to be ongoing, ambiguous in impacts or even generally regarded as not going well.

The process needs to be accessible, flexible, stimulating and even enjoyable. Large anchor institutions involved in leadership, governance, and management of inclusion and innovation are complex organisations with sometimes competing priorities and accountabilities. To take time out to reflect, deliberate, and build shared understandings and trust on deeply entrenched, often longstanding, systemic problems is not a trivial undertaking. Finally, in terms of principles, although the approach is flexible and adaptive, it needs to have enough consistency and read across to generate insights and learning points between innovation districts and places with different contexts and cultures.

This set of collaboration principles can be structured in the form of a "collaborative research and consultancy product" in its own right. The next section outlines how this product was created and developed in the i3o programme. Regardless of whether the specific i3o processes and tools are deployed, we believe these principles will increase the prospects of substantial and embedded progress in inclusive innovation policy development in contexts and cultures beyond the four cities with which the i3o programme has collaborated to date.

3.3 THE PROCESS IS THE PRODUCT

The process consultancy approach outlined in Figure 3.2 can meet many of the good practice principles relevant to dealing with multi-agency and multi-territorial "wicked issues". The process is replicable and comparable across places, within the limitations and constraints of each innovation district and its location. It can be adapted for local context and culture and has in practice evolved with lessons from each successive case. It is intentionally a light touch methodology, to provide flexibility for adaptation across a range of innovation district types and geographic contexts. It can be undertaken quickly, in lapsed time if necessary, and at a level of detailed inquiry in scale and scope determined by the participating places and institutions.

Figure 3.2 The Improving Inclusive Innovation Outcomes (i3o) case study methodology

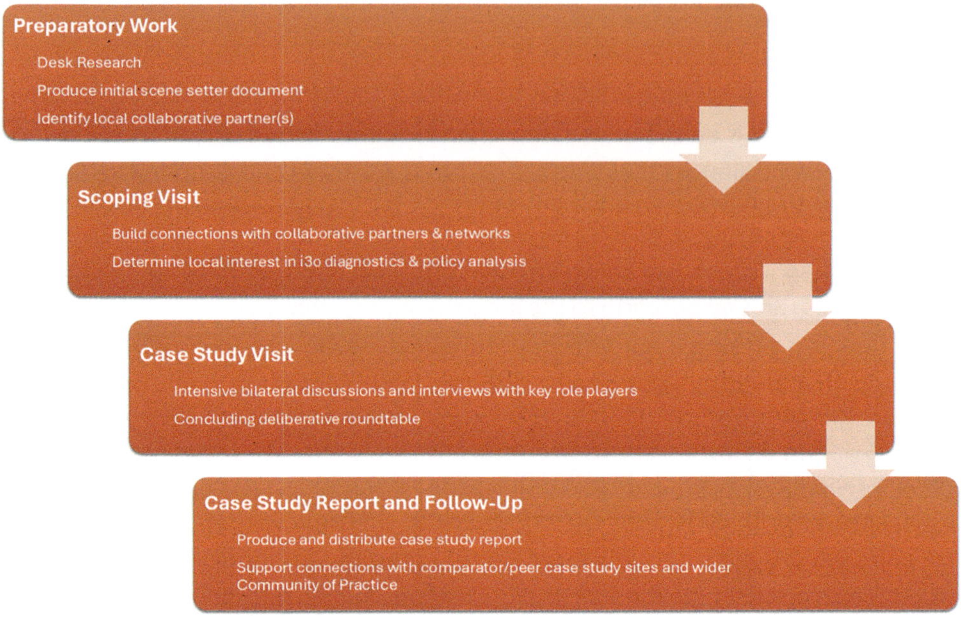

Initial desk research by the independent facilitators produces a scene-setter document of the city's recent history, the evolution of its innovation ecosystem and innovation district(s), which is shared with a wide range of role-players to sense-check. An initial scoping visit discusses the scene-setter and establishes connections with the host innovation district and city-region. It tests the appetite amongst policymakers and their delivery partners for inclusive innovation policy development, the parameters of any full i3o case study exercise and the identification of local collaborator – usually someone from a local university. It introduces them to the detailed methodology and determines how it can be applied appropriately in their city.

The local collaborator is an inclusive innovation role-player as part of the innovation ecosystem, yet who can also play a semi-independent facilitator role as a full member of the i3o team. This increases the potential for continuity and follow-up following the case study visit.

Managing the actual and perceived conflicts of interest that Schein suggests might disqualify local universities from playing this role.[3] The university as "neutral convenor" is an important place-based policy development function,[4] increasingly being undertaken in practice.[5] In the i3o case, besides the local university's own discipline in transparency, separation of roles and academic integrity, they are one member of an international disciplinary team. This enables the benefits of local embeddedness and ownership of findings to minimise any concerns on conflicts of interest.

Full case study fieldwork is typically carried out over a week by four to five team members. It comprises 15–25 bilateral interviews with a breadth of anchor institutions and role-players, along with "walking the walk" immersion in the local footprints of the innovation district and local communities. A facilitated, deliberative policy roundtable at the end of the week with interviewees and other key role-players shares and sense-checks the initial findings and discusses emerging issues.

Finally, a position paper summarising the case is produced to inform future innovation policy development in the innovation district and the city. Each innovation district and city is offered an opportunity for follow-up networking and exchange of experience with other i3o cities as part of an i3o community of practice, an offer all four cities have taken up (Figure 3.3).

There are issues that are always going to be challenging to resolve with this approach. For example, agreeing the communities of place and interest that will be in scope, and giving opportunities for their voices to be heard, is always going to involve compromises. This was

Figure 3.3 Reciprocal policy exchange in Medellín, Colombia, December 2025.

Photo: Diana Morales

particularly the case in Pittsburgh, where the neighbouring community is intimately engaged in some specific aspects of the innovation district's development, while other communities potentially impacted, but further afield, have very limited or no involvement.

In a similar vein, defining spatial, systemic and policy boundaries need to be considered. Is the focus the innovation district and adjacent neighbours, the wider urban system, the region, or all three? In Medellín, for instance, is the city's reinvention as impactful in the wider metro-region and Antioquia province as it could be? How far should inclusive innovation enquiry be contained within the innovation ecosystem, or should it consider skills, employment, enterprise and wider policy agendas? In all four cities, the skills and enterprise agendas are arguably as critical as the innovation ecosystem. This can be a challenge for the pivotal roles of the universities in the innovation district.

These questions should be considered by future places conducting this sort of exercise. But the deliberative character of the approach helps build trust to determine these issues. That case studies' choices may end up being tactical and opportunistic is not fatal to the process. The case study exercise is intended to be catalytic. Understandings and collateral that emerge from it may subsequently inform innovation district business strategy and place-based consideration of STRI contributions to inclusive growth.

3.4 TOOLS AND FRAMEWORKS

The structuring of the four inclusive innovation case studies deployed a common set of tools, frameworks, and devices to inform deliberation and policy development.

3.4.1 Tool 1: Strategic positioning matrix

Tool 1 can be used both descriptively and prescriptively to plot inclusive innovation activity and impact. It mainly serves to enable inclusive innovation role-players to recognise the distinction between purposeful and incidental inclusive innovation. Inclusive innovation-rich interventions will be purposeful, defining their mission, at least in part, in inclusion terms. They will robustly plan and manage interventions to deliver ambitious impacts and outcomes, ideally in each element of inclusive innovation as we have defined it in terms of outcomes, benefit distribution and agency/involvement (see Chapter 5) (Figure 3.4).

A purposeful innovation district or STRI policy can be focused on meeting societal challenges while also growing the local economic and business growth ecosystem. Even where STRI interventions do not explicitly pursue inclusive outcomes, policymakers and reviewers should still seek to be aware of incidental opportunities for local involvement and the impact they are having with and on local business and communities.

Figure 3.4 Tool 1: The strategic positioning matrix

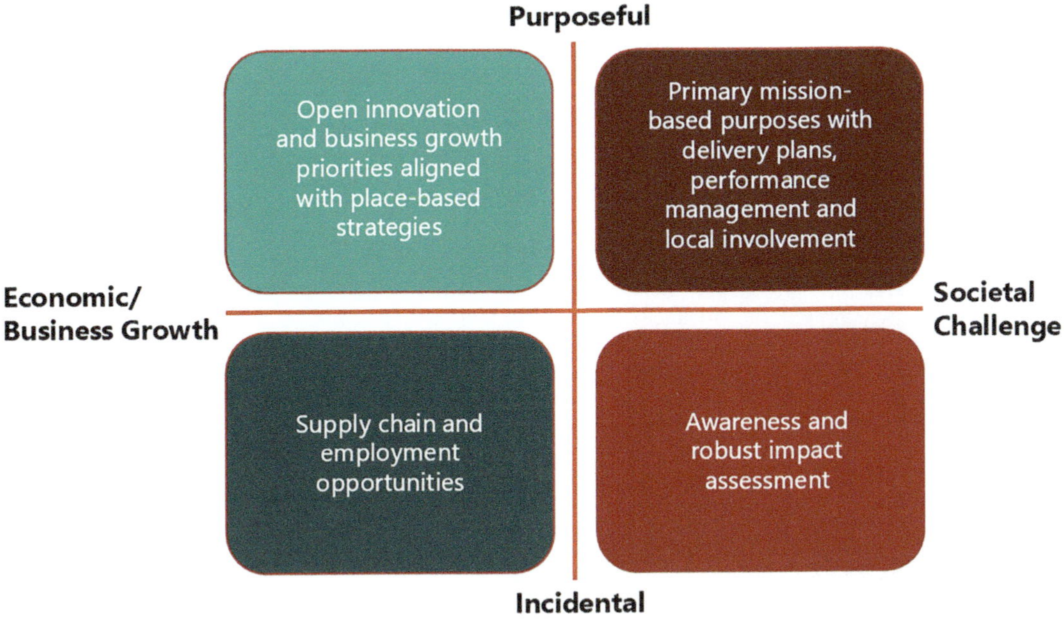

Tool 1 is primarily a mapping tool. Users of the tool should expect to have some activities in each quadrant. But it is helpful to identify what these are and the balance of activity between the different quadrants.

Figure 3.5 illustrates the sorts of issues that might populate the quadrants of the strategic positioning matrix in a specific innovation district or its wider hinterland. In the spirit of "the process is the product", periodic multidisciplinary, multi-agency exercises to populate the matrix – ideally involving a "quadruple helix" of role-players[6] – can be an aid to strategic planning and management. It can identify evidence and intelligence deficits in incidental operations, for example, tenants and operators in the innovation district who do not typically track their local relationships and impacts. It can be used to clarify, codify, and develop purposeful inclusive innovation goals and targets to redress deficits and imbalances going forward.

3.4.2 Tool 2: Rapid appraisal framework

Tool 2 is a framework for describing the innovation district's interventions (Figure 3.6). It is not meant to be a formal evaluative instrument but instead a way to stimulate thinking and debate for participants in each city's innovation ecosystem. It works on the basis that one might expect innovation districts with interests in inclusive innovation to be able to engage in discussions on the topics implied by the five questions: vision and values; goals; performance management; scalability; agency and involvement.

Figure 3.5 Goals and strategies through the strategic positioning matrix

Strategic Positioning Matrix Quadrant	Illustrative Goals/Purposes	Illustrative Intervention Strategies
PURPOSEFUL/SOCIETAL	Reduce inequalities and polarisation in local and wider communities Mitigate gentrification and displacement externalities	R&D programmes explicitly addressing inequality and liveability issues Community-driven research programmes integral to innovation district development and operations
PURPOSEFUL/ECONOMIC	Increase productivity and innovation in foundation sectors and industries Supply chain/employment opportunities for local firms and communities	Research, Development and Innovation focus on foundation sectors and industries Explicit supply chain, employment, skills and training progression programmes
INCIDENTAL/SOCIETAL	Encourage mixed social uses (including housing) and innovation district access for local communities and non-traditional users	Policies and programmes that address barriers to access and make the innovation district a genuine part of the city's urban living
INCIDENTAL/ECONOMIC	Promote social value, 'good jobs', real living wage (UK), and other standards across the innovation district	Consider and promote values in the curation and performance management of the innovation district

Figure 3.6 Tool 2: The rapid assessment framework

Rapid Appraisal Questions	G	A	R	Evidence/Examples/Comments
Do primary purposes address explicit societal and environmental challenges?				Vision, Values and Mission Statements Other Purposes
Are 'SMART' goals set for inclusive growth, social and environmental improvement?				Business Plans and Strategies Other Goals and Target-Driven Material
Are inclusion impacts (purposeful and incidental) measured?				Performance Management System Impact Assessment & Evaluation Exercises
How readily are inclusion impacts scaleable up and out?				Translation, Adoption, Commercialization
How involved are local communities and companies?				Local Engagement in Strategy & Operations Access to Facilities & Expertise Local Beneficiaries, including Supply Chains Corporate Social Responsibility Activity

The rapid appraisal framework can be used as a checklist for bilateral interviews. It can also create a "traffic light" assessment for the five topics of analysis in round table discussions or the case study final report. It might contribute to more forensic analysis and lines of enquiry for detailed inclusive growth and wider place-based strategies.

While the questions are generic, they can be tailored for local circumstances and priorities. For example, where a city or region has an adopted an explicit inclusive growth strategy, this should be used as a starting point for informing the indicators of achievement for the framework. Where investors or government funders attach specific metrics to their investments and programmes, it may be helpful to consider how far these are relevant and important metrics for the inclusive innovation outcomes sought locally. The fourth and fifth questions on scalability and community agency are more qualitative, but are good open "starters" to deeper conversations about the place-specific networks and capacities that would shape actionable policies to improve inclusive innovation.

3.4.3 Tool 3: Dos and don'ts

Tool 3 offers some rules of thumb for policy and practice. Having deployed the strategic positioning matrix and rapid appraisal framework to stimulate consideration of the policy and practice of inclusive innovation, it is possible to elaborate high-level "rules of thumb" for policy and practice development, based on the insights revealed during the case study. The

Figure 3.7 The dos and don'ts for inclusive innovation

Do create explicit inclusion targets as early as possible and embed them in the goals and purposes of the programme or project. Find compromises and champion win-win scenarios.	**Don't** avoid difficult questions about trade offs between different strategic and policy goals. There won't be a single right answer.
Do build relevant inclusion indicators of success into the operational performance management, monitoring and evaluation intelligence systems of the programme or project, starting with a clear baseline.	**Don't** hold off on designing early inclusion dimensions on the grounds that issues like physical build or financial stability haven't been achieved. Sequencing isn't necessarily linear!
Do agree upon 'touchpoints' for communities of place and interest at an early stage, and determine opportunities where they can lead and/or manage the programme or project.	**Don't** sacrifice inclusive growth values to other demands: stand firm! Be clear about the benefits of inclusion and seek offsets where compromise is needed.
Do ensure the intervention aligns and connects to wider city-region strategic priorities with links to local ecosystems (innovation, infrastructure, community, enterprise, and workforce development). Ensure that new independent and constructive voices can enter the conversation.	**Don't** allow 'Ivory Tower' cultures or priorities to create barriers to access and involvement unless there are very strong arguments that can be explained to those who will be excluded.
Do promote core inclusion and sustainability-driven standards; proactively curate activity in the programme or project that can drive and assure positive inclusion impacts.	**Don't** let debates over inclusive innovation be dominated by the 'usual suspects' of the local inclusion and innovation communities.

case study approach is likely to surface issues that have been dealt with well and progressed inclusion-rich activity and outcomes, as well as those that have been less positive.

Case study participants or even a wider leadership group can extrapolate from the case study and their own experience a small number of "dos and don'ts" of inclusive innovation relevant to their local area. An example of five dos and don'ts drawn from a synthesis of the four case studies is shown in Figure 3.7, which demonstrates how this exercise can summarise in an accessible, usable format some simple principles of better inclusive innovation. It also suggests that these principles travel well. Comparing a local dos and don'ts listing with other cities or with a synthesis template is a valuable exercise for local leadership teams. Applying it thereafter can be a helpful starting point for future policy and practice development.

Of course, these are not the only tools that have been proposed for appraising and managing inclusion activity and impacts of STRI and innovation district initiatives. For instance, the UK Innovation Districts Group (UKIDG)/Connected Places Catapult "Design, Delivery and Diffusion" framework[7] provides a more detailed framework consistent with the i3o definition

Figure 3.8 Framework for action: leadership, engagement, alignment

Actionable Insight	The i3o Inclusive Innovation Definition		
	Outcomes	Benefits Distribution	Agency and Involvement
Leadership and Management	Do STRI interventions seek to address specific local economic and social challenges?	Do we measure and try to manage how STRI benefits are distributed?	What role do local communities of place and interest perform in prioritization and decision-making?
	Are there synergistic linkages and progression pathways between the specific STRI intervention strategy, the wider STRI ecosystem, and other development and change priorities...and especially for less-advantaged communities of place and practice?		
Community Engagement and Placemaking	What is in scope and out of scope for wider public access? Are there 'Living Lab' components to the initiative, or to components within it?	Can local businesses and communities use spaces in the innovation district? Do changes in the area's character give tangible benefits to local communities?	Can local businesses and communities influence hos spaces in the innovation district are used? Do local communities consider that they have some ownership of the STRI spaces and activities?
Strategic Alignment and Territorial Equity	How do STRI agendas help delivery of city/regional strategic priorities?	Is there a menu of supply chain, education and skills, and other inreach/outreach?	How do we respond to the articulated needs of local businesses and communities?
	Have wider city-region and regional impacts been considered and included? How do communities of interest outside the local area get involved in the innovation district?		

and tools. The i3o programme team continues to develop versions of its rapid appraisal framework (Figure 3.8) that meet the needs of individual cities and their innovation districts.

The three primary tools in this chapter are proposed for their simplicity and usability for a breadth of settings and purposes.

3.5 CONCLUSIONS

The main takeaway from this chapter is that a tried-and-tested case study approach deploying relatively accessible and simple tools and frameworks can be used to bring the inclusive innovation theme to practical application. As an analytic framework, it enables diagnosis of the current inclusion-richness of an innovation district. As a collaborative research and consultancy exercise, it assists in the design and development of future innovation district priorities and practice. The following chapters demonstrate the approach in four innovation districts.

NOTES

1 These principles draw on Edgar Schein's foundational work on process consultation: Schein, E (1969) *Process Consultation: Lessons for Managers and Consultants.* Addison-Wesley Publishing Company. We deployed process consultancy techniques, including adaptive leadership mindsets and systems thinking, to help the innovation district leadership teams and partners think about how to strengthen inclusive innovation outcomes. Collaborative governance moves beyond traditional hierarchical (top-down) or market-based (private sector) solutions to achieve improved inclusion outcomes. Many actors and organisations must work deliberately together over the medium and long terms if innovation district leaders are to deliver enduring, sustainable, inclusion-rich progress to their city-region.

2 Rittel HWJ and Webber MM (1973) Dilemmas in a general theory of planning. *Policy Sciences*, 4(2): 155–169. https://urbanpolicy.net/wp-content/uploads/2015/06/Rittel-Webber_1973_DilemmasInAGeneralTheoryOfPlanning.pdf

3 Schein (1969), see Reference 1.

4 Henderson D, Morgan K and Delbridge R (2024) Putting missions in their place: Micro missions and the role of universities in delivering challenge-led innovation. *Regional Studies*, 58(1): 208–219. https://doi.org/10.1080/00343404.2023.2176840

5 Kempton L, Marlow D and Tewdwr-Jones M (2019) *Inclusive Future Growth in English Cities and Regions: Realising the Transformational University Dividend?* Newcastle City Futures.

6 See Chapter 2 for an explanation of the quadruple helix concept.

7 UKIDG (2022) *Opening the Innovation Economy: The Case for Inclusive Innovation in the UK* (Report). UKIDG & Connected Places Catapult.

4. Comparing inclusive innovation in post-industrial and post-conflict innovation districts

4.1 INTRODUCTION

This chapter provides an overview of the four case study cities and their innovation districts. Each city featured in this Policy Impact book is at a different stage of an innovation journey that leaders hope will deliver meaningful social and physical transformation of the innovation district sites and maximise economic impact for the surrounding communities, city and region. Taken collectively, the city cases represent different experiments toward an anticipated future best practice model that we term "Innovation Districts 2.0", since all four cases centre a commitment to inclusive innovation as part of their strategic vision. Based on the research described in Chapter 2, we defined inclusive innovation as *the co-creation of new ideas, practices or technologies with local communities, businesses and organisations to address societal challenges, ensuring equitable benefit distribution and fostering community empowerment* that is invariably shaped by geographical context and local priorities. Our Improving Inclusive Innovation Outcomes (i3o) research selected the four case study cities to test the premise that place matters, matching two pairs of cities according to the broader transformations underway within them.

The i3o project began by selecting two post-industrial cities where innovation districts were being developed with strong involvement by local research universities. Both innovation districts were adjacent to historically marginalised neighbourhoods and residents: the West End in Newcastle (England, UK) (Figure 4.1), and Hazelwood in Pittsburgh (PA, USA) (Figure 4.2). These developments are both aspirational, featuring high-quality placemaking, and yet each raises the concern of whether the large-scale investments in knowledge-based industries might increase the urban inequalities that have existed since the collapse of traditional manufacturing in these cities. Newcastle and Pittsburgh each have legacies of traditional industry, with local community pride based in the hands-on activities that used to occur in coal mines, steel mills, shipyards or other factories (Box 4.1). Each city has changed greatly since the late 20th century as manufacturing left and former industrial land became vacant and abandoned. Newcastle and Pittsburgh are fortunate to have transformed since then, and new economic strategies have emerged that took advantage of the research-focused universities located there. The historic focus on urban manufacturing is turning toward a new focus on knowledge as a raw material, with innovation districts and science, technology and research-led innovation (STRI) at the centre of this urban change. Some academic debates still exist about whether cities are ever truly post-industrial,[1] but regardless of the label, both Newcastle and Pittsburgh are cities affected by real personal and regional trauma for residents who have seen that urban change happen around them, and the new innovation districts replacing one urban identity with something else entirely.[2]

Our team also wanted to understand how inclusive innovation policy is creating new practices in different regional circumstances, so we chose to examine two cities emerging from periods of significant structural violence. Violence is a different form of personal and regional trauma

https://doi.org/10.1080/2578711X.2026.2624326

Figure 4.1 Scaled map of Newcastle upon Tyne and the Helix

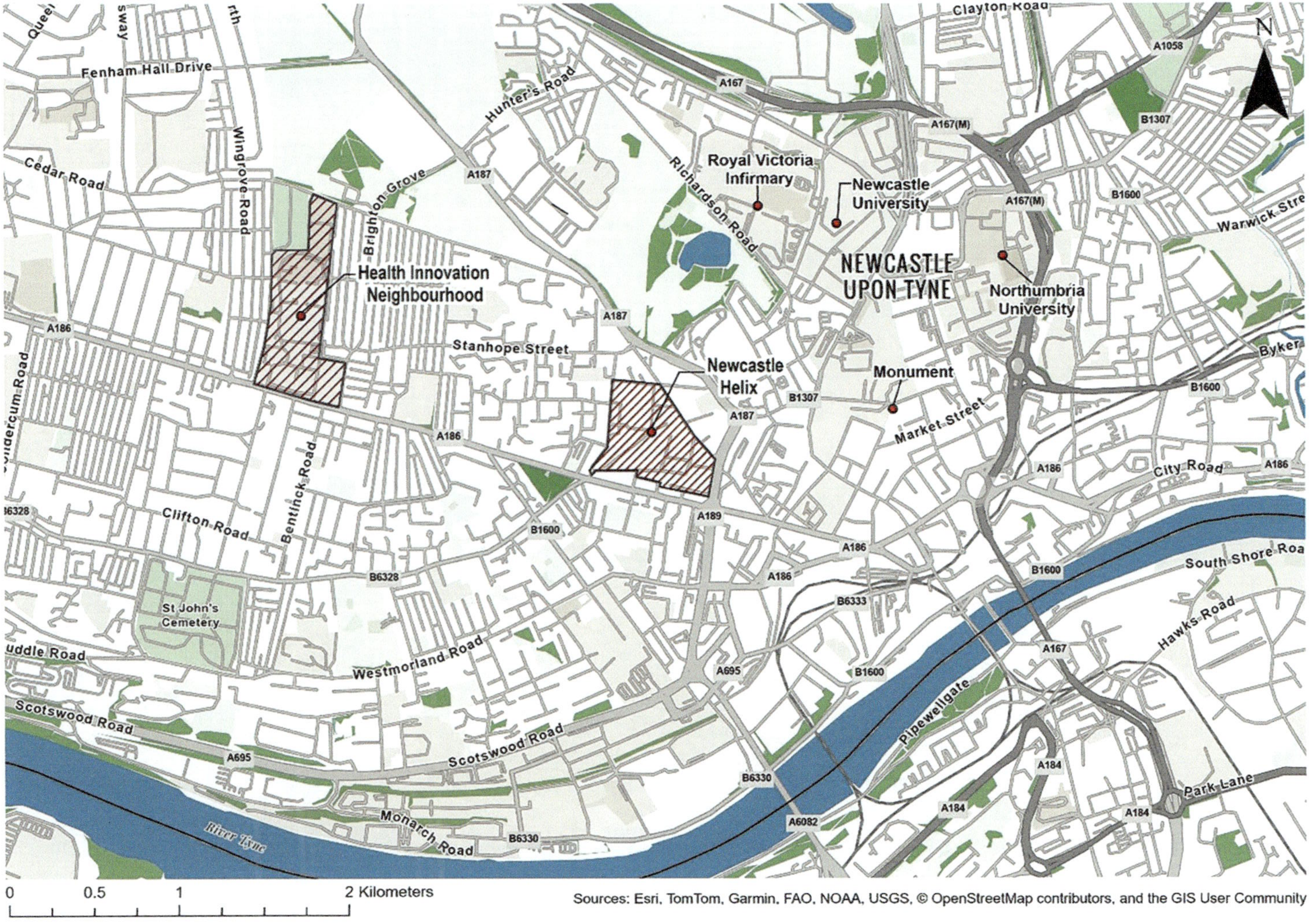

Figure 4.2 Scaled map of Pittsburgh and the Hazelwood Green innovation district (HGID)

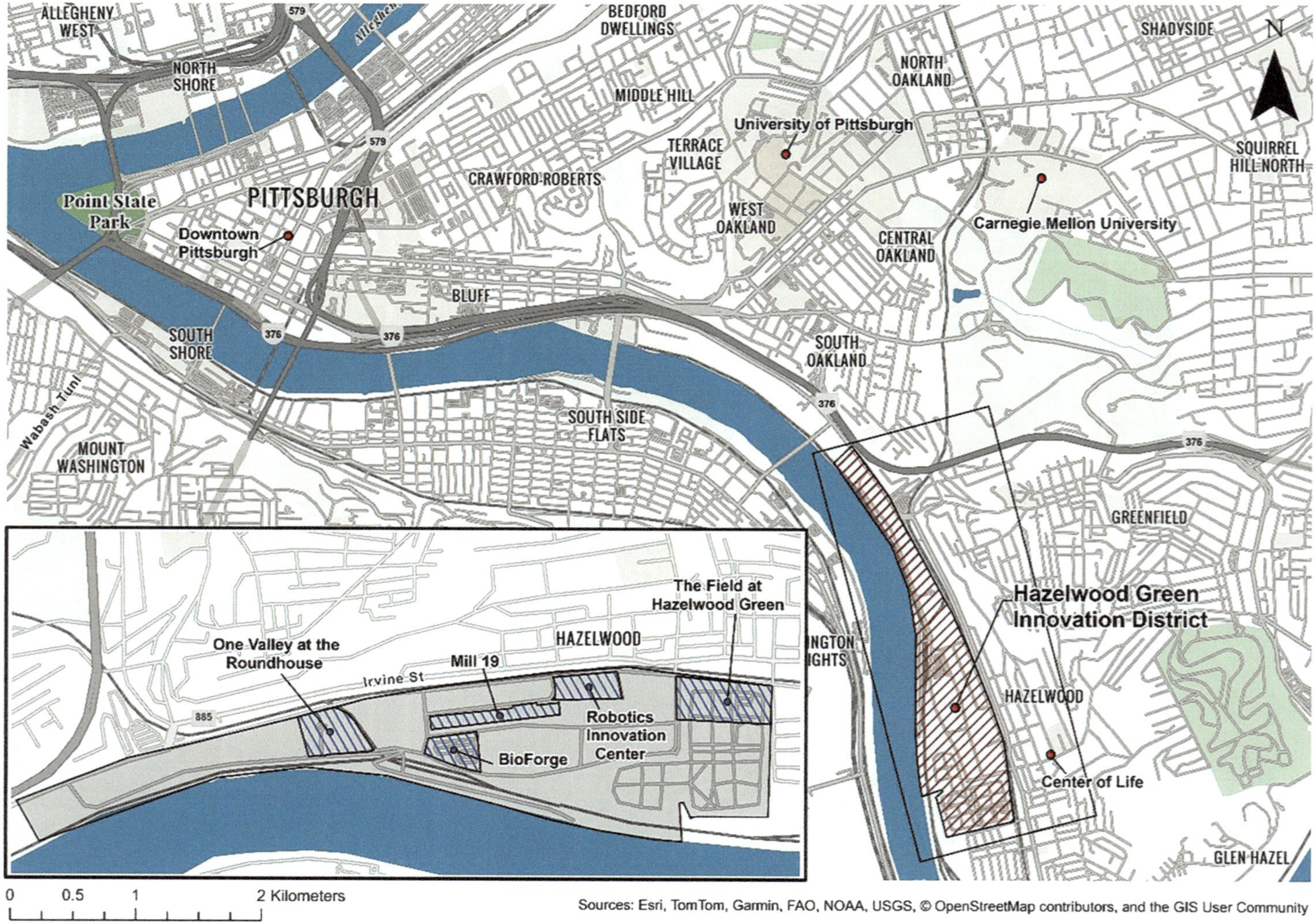

Box 4.1: Belfast's Transformation:

Following the Good Friday peace accords and boosted by Ireland's economic boom during the 2000s, Belfast underwent a significant economic transformation. The city's economy has evolved to focus on financial services, becoming a major hub for banking, insurance and other financial sectors. Belfast became a core centre for back-office operations, which led to the development of a local cybersecurity cluster. Additionally, there has been growth in the creative industries and information technology, particularly information security. Belfast had – led by the Harbour Board and a local property development company – developed a Northern Ireland Science Park in the Titanic Quarter. City leaders subsequently fostered a city-wide innovation ecosystem that leveraged the universities to create a polycentric model with key city centre and city-region nodes, including the Catalyst. The city's City Deal and a city innovation strategy with a focus on digital technologies was subsequently linked to broader regeneration of the city centre.

from that of deindustrialisation and creates long-lasting effects on the image of cities and on how residents experience them.[3] We selected Medellín (Colombia) and Belfast (Northern Ireland, UK) as internationally recognised cases that are emerging from different types of long-lasting urban conflict. Medellín's history of armed conflict centred on violence between armed organisations during the 1980s–90s. The physical layout of the city meant that poor neighbourhoods were physically isolated and vulnerable to violence (Figure 4.3). Belfast's history of conflict involved struggles between different social and religious groups, and the city became physically divided by walls and barricades that separated rival groups, creating divisions that last into the present (Figure 4.4). Innovation-based policy is now being used to unite each of these divided cities: but does this benefit the most marginal communities and residents?

The remainder of this chapter describes how each city is at a different stage of the "inclusive innovation" journey and explains how placemaking is fostering a new identity that is moving beyond deindustrialisation and/or structural violence to promise something new. Chapter 5 follows by discussing the key insights for inclusive innovation arising from this comparative case study research; Chapter 6 will outline the policy prescription for other cities that want to develop their own inclusive innovation pathway.

4.2 THE BENEFITS OF CITY COMPARISON

Bringing these four cities together to explore the birth of a new "Innovation District 2.0" model based on inclusive innovation provides the chance to understand how different leadership coalitions are approaching the promise of inclusion to deliver greater impacts for place-based investment. Newcastle and Pittsburgh are similarly sized cities with central city populations of approximately 300,000 residents and broader metropolitan populations of

Figure 4.3 Scaled map of Medellín and Ruta N

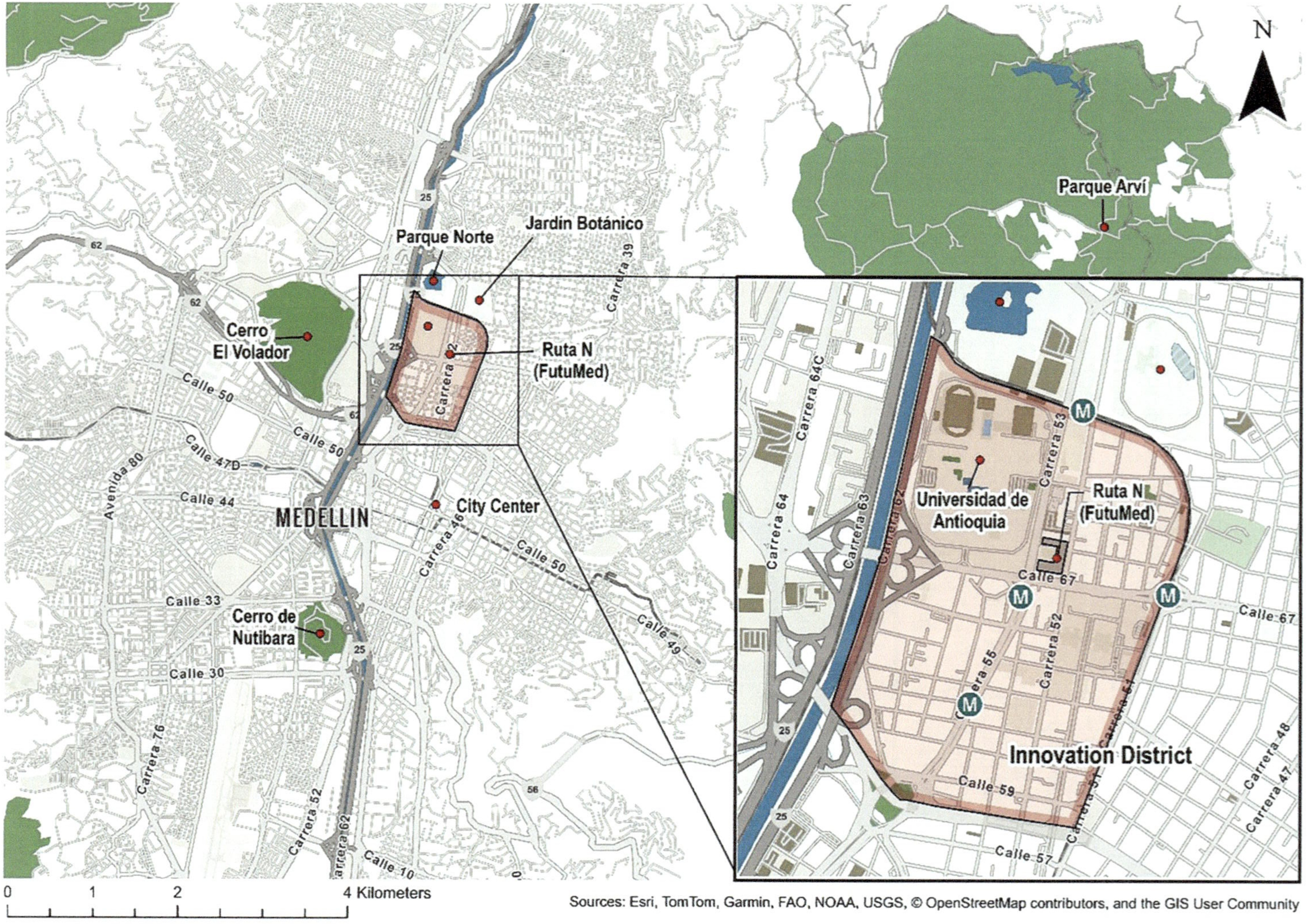

Sources: Esri, TomTom, Garmin, FAO, NOAA, USGS, © OpenStreetMap contributors, and the GIS User Community

Figure 4.4 Scaled map of Belfast and the innovation ecosystem

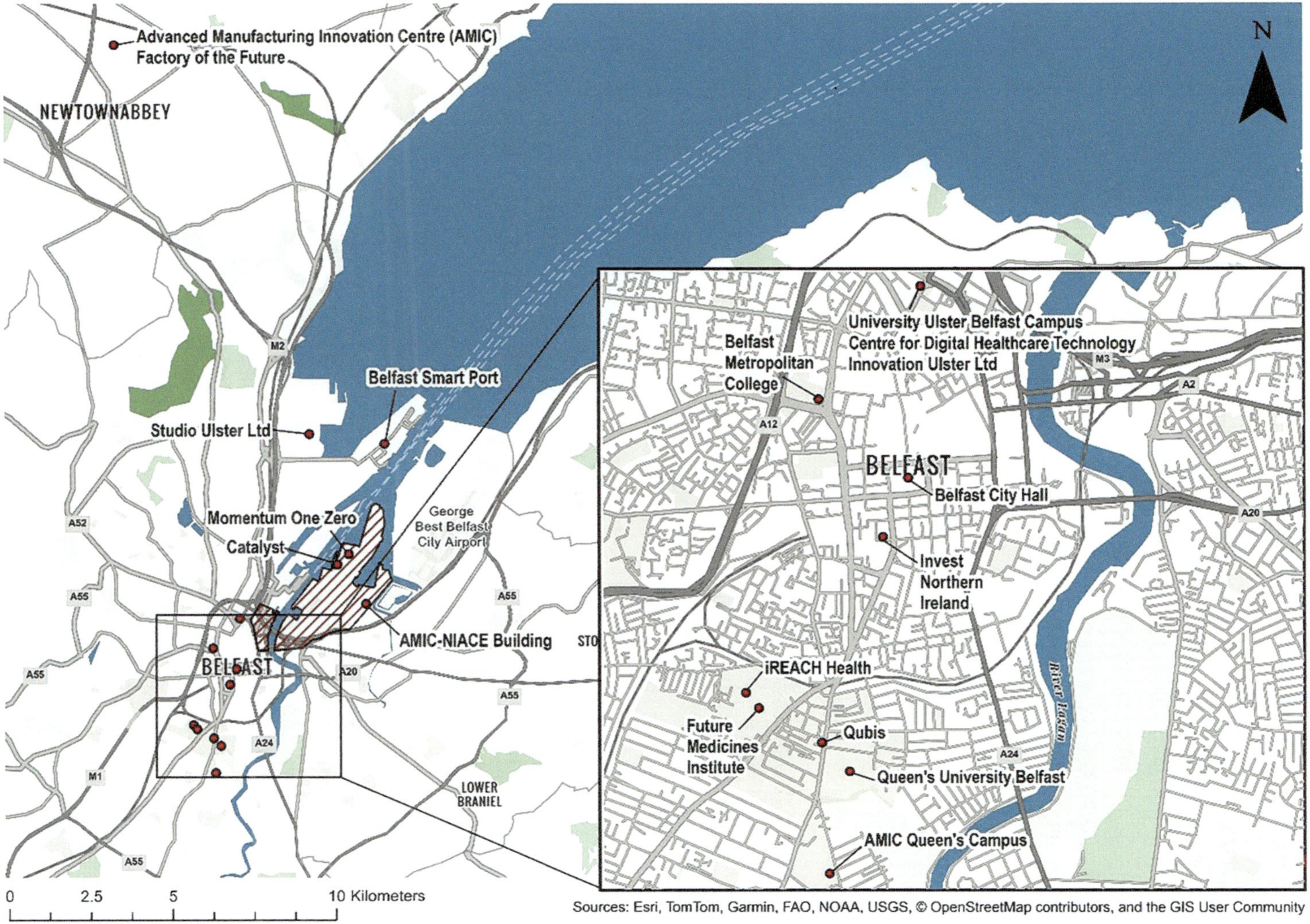

Sources: Esri, TomTom, Garmin, FAO, NOAA, USGS, © OpenStreetMap contributors, and the GIS User Community

1.7 million (Newcastle) and 2.3 million (Pittsburgh). Both regions were dominated by heavy industry (coal mining and shipbuilding in Newcastle; steel production and related manufacturing in Pittsburgh) from the 18th to the late 20th centuries when each city (and its hinterlands) experienced rapid economic disinvestment and significant population decline. Each city is leveraging its legacy as an economic centre and its existing assets in higher education and research-led healthcare to develop new post-industrial narratives as a centre of knowledge-based growth. The i3o programme has researched the innovation districts under development in each city, which share a common circumstance in that they are each built on revitalised brownfield land located near to university precincts. Our selection of two regions recovering from structural urban violence adds a further dimension to our analysis. Urban violence is shown to destabilise urban function, realigning governance arrangements and reducing urban social resilience. Belfast represents a prominent UK-based example of a city affected by multiple generations of urban violence, while Medellín provides an example of post-conflict urbanism that shows how the practice of inclusive innovation looks in a city in a middle-income country of the Global South.

Each city includes a different mix of private, public and civil society actors, yet all are linked by a shared strategy to use inclusive innovation in ways that make sense for their specific urban situation. We argue that narratives of inclusive innovation as a "fuzzy" or imprecise concept overlooks the similarities in how inclusion is factored into urban innovation policies, and by pairing these case studies we show how policymakers in different urban contexts can learn from one another's experiences in attempting to create urban transformation through inclusive innovation policies. The following sections describe the four cases as they move through three different phases (triggers for reinvention, evolution of the ecosystem and towards "Innovation District 2.0"), highlighting how inclusive innovation evolved in each city and phase.

4.3 TRIGGERS FOR REINVENTION IN THE i3o CITY CASES

There are common elements linking the four cities in this study. For instance, each uses the knowledge economy and innovation as a policy goal to spur wider urban transformation. These commonalities are perhaps most apparent in the period before each city broke ground on their innovation districts. In Medellín's case, the city's recent history is connected to Colombia's broader post-conflict path. Once known globally for its violence, Medellín experienced a profound social and economic breakdown during the 1980s–90s because of narcotrafficking, high homicide rates and the entanglement of local dynamics with the internal armed conflict. In 1991, Medellín reached a record-high homicide rate of 381 violent deaths per 100,000 inhabitants, making it one of the most dangerous cities in the world.[4] However, Medellín was not always defined by violence. Historically an industrial powerhouse – fuelled by its textile, footwear and manufacturing sectors – the city only began to decline in the 1970s due to structural weaknesses, disinvestment and lack of technological modernisation.[5] This political vacuum led to the rise of criminal networks and urban poverty. Medellín began a decades-long transformation following the death of the drug lord Pablo Escobar in 1993. The city's leadership moved to a strong social urbanism model that local leaders achieved by sustained institutional strengthening, building multisector partnerships and creating a long-term vision for social recovery. Local government, universities and the private sector converged around a shared agenda to address violence, inequality and socio-economic exclusion, linking disadvantaged communities to city growth through the provision of transportation infrastructure and laying the groundwork for what would later be recognised as a unique urban innovation model grounded in social urbanism and community participation.[6]

Newcastle upon Tyne has an economic history emblematic of broader urban decline in the North Atlantic, with 19th- and 20th-centuries growth in heavy industry turning to tragedy as international competition and domestic policy combined to cause an extended period of deindustrialisation in the 1970s–80s. Newcastle's legacy of coal mining and shipbuilding was dismantled, gradually replaced by a focus on new manufacturing sectors and the service economy. The city is home to two leading universities (Newcastle and Northumbria universities) and this presence of research activity has fostered regional growth around the medical, digital and creative sectors. Newcastle differs from Medellín because it was never as important to the UK's national economic development policy as Medellín was to Colombia, and the city's geographical separation from South East England has led to an inconsistent succession of economic development strategies. Despite this, the North East is characterised by strong local and regional governments committed to supporting the region's continued growth.

Pittsburgh's economic decline and rebirth parallels the Newcastle story in some ways, with the region's geographical isolation and overreliance on the steel industry leading to a painful collapse in the 1980s, with gradual redefinition and renewal that centred on the knowledge economy. The Pittsburgh city-region is hindered by a complex mosaic of local governments with Allegheny County alone having 130 independent municipalities, many of which emerged through industrial-era gerrymandering of company towns. There is little will to restructure this municipal system despite subsequent firm and population loss. Beyond this political fragmentation there are further complications with separate school districts, public authorities, public sector organisations and a weakened private sector that cause challenges for strategic coherence.

Unlike the other cities in the study, Pittsburgh's redevelopment has benefited from the presence of a robust philanthropic sector, with large legacy foundations providing both financial resources and unelected strategic oversight for the region. By the early 2000s, much of Pittsburgh's new economic growth came from the medical and higher education sectors which provided a new base for the regional economy and gave a new identity for city leaders to promote, often referred to as an "Eds and Meds" strategy.[7] Economic development initiatives, particularly in the city of Pittsburgh, included redeveloping former industrial sites and increasing the role of STRI through partnerships with the city's major universities, the University of Pittsburgh and Carnegie Mellon University.

4.4 DEINDUSTRIALISATION IN A GLOBAL CONTEXT

The term "post-industrial" describes the experience of all four cities in the i3o study, where all underwent profound transformations from eras in which each city was associated with heavy industry, mass production and social relations that sustained urban identities. Belfast's and Newcastle's histories as major centres for shipbuilding, coal mining (Newcastle) and textiles (Belfast), Pittsburgh's rise as a steel manufacturing centre, and Medellín's legacy as a textiles manufacturing hub were each accompanied by the construction of expansive urban landscapes that became obsolete as traditional industries closed, production shifted to other locations and city leaders began to pivot toward urban futures associated with the "knowledge economy". The decline of traditional manufacturing in each of these cities left considerable vacant land requiring redevelopment and the process of dismantling urban industrial sites began to erase physical reminders of the industrial era, clearing the way for post-industrial uses including entertainment complexes, museums and other commemorative sites, and innovation districts. Pittsburgh and Newcastle did not encounter the same structural violence as in Medellín or Belfast, but the erasure of sites such as the Jones & Laughlin steel complex in Hazelwood or the Scottish and Newcastle Brewery constituted an urban erasure that represented a community trauma of a different type. Innovation districts that are formed on the cleared sites adjacent to communities that relied on jobs in those places need to acknowledge collective memory of that past (Figure 4.5).

Figure 4.5 Demolishing the Newcastle Brewery, June 2008.

Source: Photo: smlp.co.uk. Licence provided by https://creativecommons.org/licenses/by/2.0/

Belfast features a history of industrial growth, subsequent economic decline and innovation-based renewal. Yet in the public consciousness, Belfast's urban trajectory is shaped by its history of sectarian violence and division. Belfast is the second-largest urban agglomeration on the island of Ireland, and is Northern Ireland's key centre for global connectivity. The city rose to prominence as an industrial and manufacturing city specialising in shipbuilding (famously the Titanic), textiles and ropemaking, yet was beset by a mutually reinforcing mixture of violence, deindustrialisation and depopulation from the mid-20th century. The profound geographical divisions between sectarian communities challenged the city's opportunities for renewal, and this was further challenged by Belfast's marginal political status within the UK. Signs of growth began following the 1998 Good Friday peace accords and Northern Ireland benefitted from the Republic of Ireland's economic boom during the 2000s that led Belfast to become important for back-office operations for international conglomerates and cybersecurity.

4.5 EVOLUTION OF THE ECOSYSTEMS: INCLUSIVE INNOVATION AS CATALYST

Each city's inclusive innovation journey began at a slightly different time during the period 2000–20, driven by opportunity and distinguished by the mix of local and national institutions that supported development of local innovation districts. The first city of our sample to act was Medellín, whose Ruta N district is already the subject of academic research and policy evaluation.[8] Newcastle's Helix has the next longest history and is now a fully functioning innovation district, whereas Pittsburgh's Hazelwood Green is still under construction as of 2025, and Belfast's innovation district remains in the late conceptual stages, although it builds upon an already existing, albeit geographically dispersed, urban innovation ecosystem.

At the core of Medellín's transformation into a knowledge-based city stands the Ruta N innovation district (now called FutuMED), a flagship initiative launched in 2009 to catalyse inclusive economic development through STRI. Ruta N was designed as a physical and institutional space used to support start-ups, incubate high-tech ventures and foster collaboration among universities, businesses and public institutions. This policy goal became reality in the northern part of the city where the Ruta N campus was constructed adjacent to lower income neighbourhoods; a university campus, park space and new commuter rail line linked to the city's gondola network which was significant in driving broader urban connectivity from historically marginalised communities to the site (Figure 4.6). By 2019, the district had attracted over 200 companies and institutions and had incubated the Centre for the Fourth Industrial Revolution to spearhead initiatives in artificial intelligence (AI), robotics and the Internet of Things.[9] This ecosystem reinforced Medellín's positioning as a leader in Latin America's digital transformation. The Colombian Congress designated Medellín as the first District of Science, Technology, and Innovation in 2021, granting the city greater autonomy to govern innovation policy.

Medellín's transformation is deeply shaped by its social, environmental and economic patterns. The city uses a "social urbanism" model with investment in public infrastructure, transport and education in marginalised areas to improve living conditions and foster inclusion, while embracing participatory planning to involve residents in decision-making. During this time, Medellín has also capitalised on its creative industries, becoming a hub for music, art and digital media, while shifting from traditional industry to knowledge-based sectors. This is supported

Figure 4.6 Transportation infrastructure for territorial equity in Medellín.

Photo: Metro de Medellín

by cluster strategies and regional development models aimed at driving new forms of productivity and competitiveness.[10] Medellín's embedded culture of collaboration (with and across diverse communities), policy experimentation, and civic engagement enables the city's political and community leadership to build resilience in the face of historic conflict and inequality, demonstrating how innovation can be aligned with territorial equity and urban regeneration.

Newcastle and the North East of England have secured significant benefits from investments in recent decades, largely manifested through the development of new buildings and facilities to create a physical sense that an innovation economy was underway, of which Helix is a notable example. By the early 2020s, the nagging sense that this physical STRI investment had created outcomes that disproportionately benefited highly qualified, well-paid scientists, large well-financed businesses and a few ambitious entrepreneurs led to a new strategic direction that explicitly called for inclusive innovation. This policy move became more urgent because of the experience of, and responses to, the COVID-19 pandemic and the then Conservative government's embrace of a "levelling-up" mission that channelled more economic development investment to the regions. This approach was exemplified by the Helix innovation district: a 10-ha (24.7-acre) city centre former brewery site acquired in 2005 as part of Newcastle's response to the then Labour government's Science City initiative.

Helix is in the centre of Newcastle on the former site of Newcastle Breweries, between the Central Station and St James' Park Football Stadium, and adjacent to the West End communities that are amongst the most deprived nationally, regionally and in the city. The site was purchased by a consortium of the North East Regional Development Agency (One Northeast), Newcastle City Council and Newcastle University, who intended to develop a "Science Central" to promote collaborations between researchers and innovative businesses. Regional development agencies were abolished by the Conservative-led coalition government in 2010, which, alongside the post-2008 Global Financial Crisis and subsequent austerity measures, put the plans on hold. In 2016, a new partnership between Newcastle University, Newcastle City Council and Legal & General (a UK multinational financial services and asset management company) branded Helix as a new city quarter aspiring to deliver a collaborative ecosystem and testbed for sustainable urban living. Helix is intended to be open for all, and is designed to connect business, research and communities. Incorporating more than 10 commercial and research buildings, residential plots, streets and public areas, Helix has high environmental and design standards and now houses innovation-led businesses in the life sciences, data and digital industries, and three UK National Innovation Centres: Ageing, Data and Rural Enterprise; the National Institute for Health Research; and an Innovation Observatory.

The Hazelwood Green innovation district (HGID) in Pittsburgh shows how inclusive innovation can influence marginalised communities in post-industrial cities. Hazelwood Green is a 70-ha (173-acre) former coke works site that closed in 1998. Located nearly 10 km (6.2 miles) up the Monongahela River from the city's central business district, HGID is adjacent to Hazelwood, a long-distressed community that underwent significant population loss, environmental degradation and disinvestment over a 40-year period. Hazelwood Green shares commonalities with the Helix, primarily because university leadership engages with parts of the site development in both Pittsburgh and Newcastle. One important difference between the two sites is that Pittsburgh's city government and its economic development arm, the Urban Redevelopment Authority, barely play any direct roles in the site's development. Four philanthropic foundations – Heinz, RK Mellon, Benedum and McCune, branded the ALMONO consortium for the Allegheny, Monongahela and Ohio rivers of Pittsburgh – have owned the site since 2002 and control site development with the city's two major research universities – the University of Pittsburgh and Carnegie Mellon University – acting as key partners. The site sat idle for many years while five site master plans were developed and discarded, indicating indecision amongst the ownership group, Pittsburgh's weak demand characteristics and an overly conservative approach to building on a prime river-adjacent site. The sixth master plan was approved and led to construction that began in the late 2010s (by which time the McCune Foundation had relinquished its ownership stake) with adaptive reuse of two former industrial structures.

As of late 2025, construction is nearly complete on the two large university projects. These include the University of Pittsburgh's BioForge, a specialised biomanufacturing centre, and Carnegie Mellon University's Robotics Innovation Center (RIC).[11] The foundation ownership group provided much of the development costs of these projects, including nearly US$100 million to the University of Pittsburgh for the BioForge project, US$30 million for CMU's Manufacturing Futures Institute and US$45 million for the RIC. Other developments are also planned for, or in construction on, the site, including new affordable housing that aligns with the Hazelwood neighbourhood's own strategic plan.

HGID has an explicit vision to deliver "a new model for economic development in Pittsburgh, one that is aligned with community and grounded in the principles of sustainability, equity, and inclusive economic opportunity".[12] The master plan now calls for 3500 housing units, which is almost double the number of occupied units in historic Hazelwood. For the universities, the open question is how they should collaborate with the community and how that relationship will affect HGID's development goals and community impacts. The University of Pittsburgh is committed to building a community engagement centre on Hazelwood Green that will work with community organisations and residents in several ways. However, the centre will relocate community organisations that presently occupy the prominent Centre for Life building in the historic Hazelwood neighbourhood, which will risk becoming vacant. This may represent a net loss for the neighbourhood if no new tenants can be found for the existing structure. Hazelwood's residents are active participants in the deliberations over their neighbourhood's future, and a resident-developed neighbourhood plan exists as a statement of their preferred vision for development.

For inclusive innovation through Hazelwood Green to be considered successful, the Hazelwood community's existing neighbourhood plan and its "North Star Vision" should be prioritised. The HGID site remains challenging in terms of its links to the traditional neighbourhood because of physical separation by railroad tracks and roads, and because the site feels socially distinct from the community. Both are challenges that the community recognised in its community plans and that the site's developers recognised in the six master plans commissioned by the ALMONO ownership group. A central challenge remains in encouraging the philanthropic ownership group to be transparent in their goals for the site. This partnership functions without significant oversight or collaboration with local government, which creates an opaque governance structure that affects community outcomes and posed challenges to carrying out our research; for example, one of the three foundation partners refused to engage in the i3o process at all.

Belfast is the latest adopter of inclusive innovation goals and has yet to create a distinct innovation district akin to those in the other case study cities. The city's innovation plans are catalysed by the City Deal that supports a city-wide innovation ecosystem.[13] The city appears strongly networked with engaged and committed anchor institutions across the government, business, civic and academic communities. Belfast's innovation ecosystem involves a diverse array of actors, including more autonomy as a devolved part of the UK as part of a power-sharing arrangement established by the 1998 Good Friday Agreement (for details, see Box 4.1).

The innovation ecosystem in Belfast involves a diverse array of actors. From the public sector key actors include the UK government, which has provided significant financial investment and support for various projects under the City Deal. Complementing this, the Northern Ireland Executive offers matching funding and policy support to ensure alignment with regional development goals. Six local councils within the Belfast region collaborate to develop and implement different projects (Antrim and Newtownabbey, Ards and North Down, Belfast, Lisburn and Castlereagh, Mid and East Antrim, and Newry, Mourne and Down). Key higher education partners are Queen's University Belfast, Ulster University and Belfast Metropolitan College, which contribute to research, innovation and skills development initiatives. The private sector comprises businesses and industry leaders, though their engagement has proven more difficult to ensure. Community organisations and civil society groups are also a key sector to engage to ensure that the benefits of the innovation economy are inclusive and reach disadvantaged communities. Additionally, Invest Northern Ireland, the regional economic development agency, supports innovation strategies across the city-region (Figure 4.7).

While Belfast features a broad set of actors, the innovation ecosystem is narrower in scope, focusing predominantly on employability and skills. Other critical areas are not always prioritised in innovation policies, such as supporting individuals at risk of criminality, fostering foundational economy entrepreneurship and addressing feelings of being left behind. In many cases, these aspects of inclusion are left to civil society organisations, specific university programmes and colleges to address, rather than being integrated into the core strategies and actions of Belfast's innovation ecosystem. There also appears to be a mismatch between how

Figure 4.7 Belfast city centre.

Photo: Peter Steele, March 2023

innovation is explained as an economic catalyst and how the broader inclusion objectives of public policies and programmes are defined in practical terms. For example, while public procurement and projects under the City Deal and the Smart Belfast initiatives[14] emphasise social value (which is a key element of inclusive innovation best practices), this often translates into short-term measures within Belfast, such as creating jobs or employing local workers. These efforts, though valuable, do not fully connect with the city's innovation goals to ensure long-term, inclusive participation of all sectors of society.

Another ongoing challenge in Belfast is that innovation is frequently seen as something reserved for the digital and knowledge sectors, with limited integration into sectors that cater to foundational economic needs such as healthcare, education and local (mainly small and micro-) businesses. The inclusive side of innovation is thus again confined to short-term wins, rather than fostering a longer term ecosystem that ensures equal participation and access to opportunities for all communities. This mismatch could be solved through a more integrated approach that aligns innovation goals with long-term social inclusion strategies, to help all sectors of society participate and benefit from innovation-driven growth; after all, the digital society does not exist in a vacuum and could provide benefits across the city. Finally, the short-term view of inclusive innovation in existing policy is at odds with overcoming the city's history of sectarian violence. Navigating from a society defined by conflict means tackling enduring social issues through a patient focus on multi-generational inequalities.

4.6 TOWARDS AN INNOVATION DISTRICT 2.0 MODEL: INCLUSION AS DIFFERENTIATOR

The four cities in the i3o research study share an explicit commitment to inclusive innovation. Each urban leadership coalition does so because it sees inclusion as a solution to local community and economic development problems, to enhance the impact of public investment in innovation districts and to differentiate themselves from traditional innovation districts that focused inward on the tenants of the district, ignoring the needs or opportunities that could come from a deeper engagement with the surrounding communities. None of the models is infallible, and all continue to experiment and move toward what we are terming an "Innovation District 2.0" model that thoroughly embeds inclusion goals through the planning and operation of urban innovation districts.

Medellín is the most mature innovation district in our study, and the city's strategic emphasis on "social urbanism" means that Ruta N provides valuable lessons on how to build inclusive innovation in regions undergoing deep structural change. Medellín's approach prioritises community integration, collaborative governance and context-specific strategies, and its transition into a National Special District of Science, Technology, and Innovation reflects how significant the district's model has become for national innovation strategy. This presents an opportunity to evaluate the tensions between globally driven innovation narratives and locally embedded social objectives, and growing dissimilarities between the inclusion opportunities of Medellín compared with the surrounding province of Antioquia suggests that the district might yet become a victim of its own success if it exacerbates inequality at a different geographical scale.

Meanwhile, Newcastle's Helix has yet to prove effective at addressing the stark inequalities between the West End and the rest of the city. Despite Newcastle City Council and Newcastle University's co-ownership, and the stable presence of many successful business, academic and public service tenants, the West End's socio-economic performance has tended to decrease rather than converge with national and local averages. This risk is also present in Pittsburgh, where the Hazelwood Green is geographically isolated from the rest of the city's innovation ecosystem, and where the innovation district is distinct from the residential communities of Greater Hazelwood. The patient (or conservative) approach taken to site development by the ALMONO ownership group of philanthropic foundations is occurring at a different time scale than that of local residents who have waited for a generation to see jobs return to the former mill site: and now that they are, there seems to be a skills and training mismatch that is yet to be addressed. The recency of Belfast's ambitious plans for a city-wide innovation ecosystem makes assessment more challenging, though it is clear that the innovation ecosystem's leadership clearly understands that the geographical fragmentation of communities shaped through the city's history presents a transportation challenge to broad inclusive innovation, and that the rest of Ulster province is eager to see tangible benefits from Belfast's progress as a city of innovation. Overcoming geographical divisions and building an innovation district that can create true territorial equity across the city's neighbourhoods will be important for maximising the potential of the city's inclusion goals.

NOTES

1 Luger J and Schwarze T (2024) Leaving post-industrial urban studies behind? *Dialogues in Urban Research*, 2: 188–209. https://doi.org/10.1177/27541258241230058; Glass MR (2024) Whither the post-industrial city? *Dialogues in Urban Research*, 2: 214–217. https://doi.org/10/1177/27541258241262282

2 Deitrick S and Glass M (2022) Confronting the Pittsburgh narrative: Renaissance, renewal, and the tension of authenticity. In A Cole, A Healy and C Morel Journel (Eds.), *Constructing Narratives for City Governance: Transnational Perspectives on Urban Narratives* (pp. 17–30). Cheltenham: Edward Elgar.

3 Glass M, Seybolt TB and Williams P (2022) *Urban Violence, Resilience and Security: Governance Responses in the Global South*. Cheltenham: Edward Elgar.

4 Russo S (2020) *The Transformation of Crime in Medellín, Colombia*. The Borgen Project. https://borgenproject.org/crime-in-medellin-colombia/

5 Franz T (2017) Urban governance and economic development in Medellín: An "urban miracle"? *Latin American Perspectives*, 44(2): 52–70. https://doi.org/10.1177/0094582X16668315

6 Organisation for Economic Co-operation and Development (OECD) (2015) *The Innovation Imperative: Contributing to Productivity, Growth and Well-Being*. OECD Publ. https://doi.org/10.1787/9789264239814-en

7 Deitrick and Glass (2022), see Reference 2.

8 Morisson A and Bevilacqua C (2018) Beyond innovation districts: The case of Medellín Innovation District. *Conference Paper*. ResearchGate. https://www.researchgate.net/publication/323285702; University Industry Innovation Network (UIIN) (2019) *Ruta N Transcends the Boundaries of Innovation in Colombia*. https://www.uiin.org/2019/10/03/ruta-n-transcends-the-boundaries-of-innovation-in-colombia/

9 UIIN (2019), see Reference 8.

10 Sociable (2021) *Colombia's Innovation Landscape: An Interview with Ruta N Director Iván Castaño*. https://sociable.co/technology/colombias-innovation-landscape-an-interview-with-ruta-n-director-ivan-castano/

11 Hazelwood Green is attractive to the two research universities because of the abundant vacant land it includes. While Oakland is home to the "Pittsburgh Innovation District" (PID), this district was conceived of in 2017, following recommendations by the Brookings Institution. The PID is a rebrand of an area that was already developed, whereas the Hazelwood Green provided the chance to research a purpose-built innovation district with a different (foundation-led) governance model.

12 Hazelwood Green (2025) *Hazelwood Green: The Vision*. https://hazelwoodgreen.com/

13 City deals are packages of funding and decision-making powers negotiated between central government and local UK authorities through an initiative of the UK government that began in 2012.

14 The Smart Belfast plan is an urban innovation programme using technology and data science to address city challenges. It centres on a "Smart District" in Belfast's city centre that test beds new solutions to urban problems.

5. How to build an Innovation District 2.0

5.1 INTRODUCTION

Innovation matters to community and economic development, but how can it be made more inclusive? Our Improving Inclusive Innovation Outcomes (i3o) research programme has engaged with policymakers, community representatives and development experts in four different innovation ecosystems that take inclusion seriously, and where innovation policy continues to evolve. We have found that global challenges, technological advances and a better understanding of how innovation districts can support and sustain their host cities are driving current experimentation toward a new type of innovation district.

Belfast, Pittsburgh, Medellín and Newcastle all reflect elements of an emerging "next practice" toolkit for cities wanting to be globally competitive through promoting the knowledge economy and innovation. Each city starts with a focus on high-quality place-making within the grounds of the innovation district that uses mixed-use developments and attractive design to attract a mix of skilled workers, investors, university researchers and private firms. The goal of this place-making is to provide a dynamic ecosystem that will spur new innovations and hopefully lead to sustained place-based growth. This is classic innovation district place-making: "Innovation Districts 1.0", and these can be found in cities across the world. Only Medellín, arguably, built in connectivity with neighbouring communities and hillside *comunas* from the start of the innovation district with its northern district mixed-use created as a city-wide destination from its start.

And yet, innovation districts continue to evolve, and our research finds that inclusive innovation is an emerging trend that we hypothesise is gradually creating what we term "Innovation Districts 2.0". These new forms of urban innovation district will use broader and more resilient indicators of success that go beyond traditional aggregate growth metrics. The four cases show that leaders of urban innovation ecosystems are using place-based developments to address societal challenges and are looking to maximise public investment in innovation districts by thinking more broadly about the ongoing work in the confines of each district. It is no longer a question of just who to bring into your innovation district: the new leaders in place-based innovation will be those who solve the issue of how to connect with people, places and organisations outside the boundary of, and particularly adjacent to, their innovation district.

Our research finds that there are similar trends across the four cities in driving the policy goals that will become the foundation for the next generation of urban innovation districts. This chapter explains this phenomenon and identifies three key features of promising inclusive innovation: an emphasis on leadership, community relationships, and strategic alignment with urban and regional policy. Chapter 6 concludes the book by explaining how other cities can join the inclusive innovation challenge and reap the benefits of an Innovation District 2.0 model.

https://doi.org/10.1080/2578711X.2025.2624328

Table 5.1 Innovation district approaches to leadership and management

	Newcastle	Pittsburgh	Medellín	Belfast
Stage of delivery	**Established**	**Established**	**Established**	**Emergent**
Nature of collaboration and leadership	University-driven collaboration between the local government, the university and investors	Foundation-led leadership, distinct from city–university partnerships	Public–private partnership	Multi-actor collaborations between public, private actors, and universities and college
Level of leadership	Identifiable leadership and management	Clear leadership by foundations through a development agreement	Political leadership shared governance across different actors	Notionally clear leadership, but in practice diffuse and informal
Collaborations outside management	Limited via formal consultative exercises	Limited	High in both design and outcome	Limited

Source: *Morales D, Green L, Marlow D, Cadena Gaitán C, Deitrick S, Glass MR and Kempton L (2025) Defining inclusive innovation: Challenges and lessons for innovation districts. Regional Studies, Regional Science, 12(1): 740–753.* https://doi.org/10.1080/21681376.2025.2543915

The Innovation District 2.0 model we see on the horizon is drawing on a rich set of academic and policy literature spanning the social and policy sciences. Although most of the research in the literature to date is based on Global North experiences, our own research suggests that Global South cases such as Medellín are influencing innovation policy in Europe and North America, and that international networks of practice and collaboration are now spreading elements of an inclusive innovation model across the world. Some of the main features of these emerging global economic development practices are summarised in Table 5.1.

The main take-away from our scan of the current state of economic development practice (Chapter 2) is an emerging shift toward inclusion and a strengths-based approach that draws on local assets to create sustained, resilient growth arising from (but not confined within) innovation districts. There is also a strong need to avoid negative outcomes of place-based development, including price pressures on long-term residents created by otherwise beneficial economic reinvestment and redevelopment. These trends and prospects have profound impacts on science, technology and research-led innovation (STRI)-based growth strategies and innovation districts. STRI-based growth is still seen as a primary strategy for national competitiveness and place-based advantage, both to sustain existing success and to catalyse turnaround and reinvention. And yet, even as national industrial strategies continue to stress the importance of creating high-tech jobs, the attention of innovation districts is turning toward making sure that "good" jobs are created that are accessible to diverse populations, that innovation benefits geographically marginalised communities, and that technological advancements do not cause greater inequalities through gentrification, job automation or expanding gaps in the infrastructures that enable innovation.

To be clear, we argue that city leaders who recognise the importance of solving social, economic and environmental challenges through innovation districts will become distinct from cities that rely on static and old-fashioned concepts of economic success. Innovation Districts 2.0 will broaden the impact of public investments in innovation districts by expanding the target zone for STRI-based growth. This includes support for social enterprises, community-led innovation and technologies designed to improve public services. There must be an increasing focus on fostering diverse and inclusive innovation ecosystems by actively working to increase participation of women, minorities and other underrepresented groups, providing equitable access to funding, mentorship and networks within innovation hubs, and working with innovation district firms to test-bed their innovations in the communities that surround them. The urgency of the climate crisis, the need for resource efficiency and the moral urgency of expanding the benefits of public investments make inclusive innovation a necessity for urban economies of the 21st century.

Urban innovation districts stand in stark contrast to the out-of-town suburban science and business parks that were common in the pre-2000 era, which created physical and social barriers to participation by local communities. Urban Innovation District 1.0 models were projects with dual STRI and urban regeneration purposes. However, this potential has not always been realised, and the local strengths of communities surrounding the districts were often ignored, creating an us/them approach that stifled economic spillover effects. What is clear from our analysis of four innovation districts is that they can deliver inclusive growth, but also that the eventual form of Innovation Districts 2.0 is still being developed, with considerable benefits awaiting those places that get it right.

The i3o project was borne out of the observation that inclusive innovation was the policy goal for several cities internationally, all of which were earnestly striving to improve the spillover effects from their place-based investments in STRI-related innovation districts. The i3o methodology and toolkit described in Chapter 3 produced actionable insights for each city (Table 5.1). Working in partnership with innovation ecosystem partners in each city created an open dialogue that is the basis for the remainder of this chapter, and the work that will occur in each city well into the future.

Neil Lee's critique of inclusive innovation was very influential in i3o's genesis.[1] He suggested that there is a gap between the potential of inclusive innovation and whether it can be achieved. He argues that inclusive innovation is a "fuzzy concept" where multiple and inconsistent meanings can make it difficult to formulate clear policies, measure progress and ensure accountability. However, we argue that the i3o toolkit and the comparative international analysis we have undertaken points to three explicit dimensions that emerging inclusive innovation hubs have in common. Leadership, management and governance; community agency and engagement; and strategic alignment and territorial equity are essential parts of the mix for cities that want to move from good to great by acknowledging the power of inclusion when it comes to STRI policy and urban innovation districts.

5.2 WHY DOES LEADERSHIP, MANAGEMENT AND GOVERNANCE MATTER TO INCLUSION GOALS?

The case studies confirm what earlier studies suggest: that the leadership dynamics and governance structures of innovation districts are crucial to determining their overall success. High-performance leadership involves several elements. First, it involves governance that is open to including diverse sectoral representation (incorporating the private and public sectors, community participants, the research sector, and a mix of mature and start-up firms). Second, district leaders understand what makes their local context special, and they look out for emerging opportunities that can enhance this contextual strength. Third, effective district management is attuned to proactively intervening, measuring and evaluating progress toward inclusive growth. Fourth, strong leadership should include an innovation district governance structure with a clear strategic vision of how socio-economic spillover effects can be extended.[2] These leadership and governance attributes are evident in high-performing Innovation District 1.0 models that prioritise standard success metrics (including occupancy rates, job creation and gross value added (GVA), along with orthodox university and technology research, development and innovation metrics), but it is especially important for districts that want to enhance their impact as centres of inclusive growth.

The four cases each claimed to champion inclusive innovation goals, yet their success will depend on how leadership, management, and governance are structured and enacted to "walk the walk". It is clear that no one innovation district has successfully built a sustainable formula for becoming the international model of an Innovation District 2.0, but recurring themes are apparent that indicate how the race will be won.

For instance, an evident tension appears in Newcastle's Helix, where economic growth is seen to be at odds with social inclusion goals. The project developed with an evolving partnership of public, private and academic actors that lacked a consistent leadership willing to prioritise inclusive innovation targets until local champions acknowledged the need to extend the district's impact beyond a narrow set of sectors and occupations.

Pittsburgh's Hazelwood Green is marked by strong leadership from the philanthropic sector, which sets a singular vision while city and regional government is markedly silent on inclusion goals for the site. The university sector largely acts as delivery agents for the philanthropic coalition that owns the site.

Belfast's innovation landscape is similarly challenged by fragmented multilevel governance and political instability, including periods without a functioning devolved government, that hinders long-term planning and strategic coherence. This context creates a gap between high-tech innovation district narratives and the needs of the foundational economy and disadvantaged communities.

Medellín's leadership is comparatively strong and visionary, and the 2000–20 period saw inclusive innovation framed as a tool for social and geographical recovery. The city's innovation district became a hub for entrepreneurship and smart specialisation, although Ruta N suffered from some setbacks to its place-based model due to both COVID-19 and local political shifts.

Each city's innovation district has a different organisational structure, according to their own institutional capacities and landscape (Table 5.2). In Newcastle, leadership and management are a collaboration between Newcastle University, the local authority and Legal & General, creating potential tension as political and academic priorities shift.

Table 5.2 Actionable insights from the Improving Inclusive Innovation Outcomes (i3o) methodology

	Newcastle	Pittsburgh	Medellín	Belfast
Leadership and management	Formulating and agreeing an explicit inclusive innovation vision; the innovation districts' purposes in progressing that vision are critical			
	Putting in place intervention strategies and performance management systems to track, review and publicise progress			
	Greater prominence of the i3o toolkit in future Helix/HIN development	Consider how ALMONO partnership accountability is strengthened locally and in Greater Pittsburgh	Consider how to adapt social urbanism ethos for the national ST&I designation and its purposes	Consolidate the ICB leadership and reconcile Northern Ireland and Belfast Inclusive Growth priorities/metrics
Community engagement and place-making	Improve access and use of public space both within Helix and build into the HIN design	Resolve gentrification and displacement fears, and wider access to the city issues	Consider roles of *comunas* and growing inward migration communities in the ST&I designation	Address community sensitivities in distribution and access to a diffuse spread of innovation nodes across the city
Strategic alignment and territorial equity	Agree explicit contributions to relevant city inclusion strategies and priorities, and consider territorial equity issues			
	Specify Helix and HIN roles in the city and North East-inclusive growth strategies	Recognise that the scale of Hazelwood Green requires specific intervention strategies for communities beyond Hazelwood and throughout the city-region	Strengthen metropolitan, Antioquia and even neighbouring province involvement in "Medellín miracle" and the ST&I designation	Explicit alignment of the Belfast Inclusive Growth Strategy with the Northern Ireland Programme for Government and clarify Belfast's science, technology and research-led innovation (STRI) contributions to Northern Ireland and even Ireland growth and development

Note: *ALMONO = a partnership between Heinz, RK Mellon, Benedum and McCune, branded the ALMONO consortium for the Allegheny, Monongahela and Ohio rivers of Pittsburgh; ICB = Innovation City Belfast, a partnership between Belfast City Council, Belfast Harbour, Catalyst, Queen's University and Ulster University; HIN = Health Innovation Neighbourhood; ST&I = science, technology and innovation.*

In Pittsburgh, the core leadership challenge is accountability and transparency, as its innovation district is owned and developed by private foundations that remain immune to shareholder or political pressure. This means that typical democratic mechanisms holding the public sector accountable are inapplicable in this context.

Belfast's leadership structure is diffuse and dependent on multistakeholder collaborations. Complicating matters further is the fact that the country has experienced periods without a devolved national government, impacting consistency and long-term planning. Medellín has a complex system of multi-actor collaborations, but leadership is clearly articulated through public–private agreements, institutional strengthening and engagement across stakeholder groups.

Medellín's transformation included different interventions over time, multi-actor collaborations, large urban infrastructure investments and a long-term innovation strategy that prioritised social innovation, social urbanism (especially connective infrastructure focusing on marginalised communities), and science and technology. Ruta N and the city's innovation system are led by the city's local authority and other key organisations. Ruta N remains a key node in mobilising and coordinating other actors in the innovation system, but its leadership lessened over time (attributed to a "rupture" in the city's tradition of political continuity). The city's innovation system is proving resilient to political, economic or other disruptions, ensuring inclusive innovation to remain as a priority, even as some respondents reflected on Ruta N's waning influence. Thus, the city's innovation system relies on a culture of collaboration, sustained consensus-building strategies, maintaining a coherent long-term vision, and a culture of innovation and problem-solving among the city's inhabitants. These findings corroborate previous research about regional innovation systems and institutional thickness in innovation ecosystems.

As discussed in our previously published article,[3] inclusive innovation requires leadership that is strategic, transparent, collaborative and socially embedded, and these qualities must be cultivated across all governance levels and institutional actors. The case studies of Newcastle, Pittsburgh, Medellín and Belfast underscore the importance of purposeful leadership and collaborative governance in advancing inclusive innovation. While each city operates within a distinct institutional context, common challenges persist, including the critical components of inclusive innovation such as ensuring community agency, avoiding enclave developments and integrating social value into innovation strategies.

The findings suggest that inclusive innovation must be embedded from the outset, with clear goals, performance indicators and cross-sector collaboration. Policymakers and practitioners should prioritise transparency and long-term planning to ensure that innovation districts contribute meaningfully to inclusive urban development. The i3o framework offers a useful and adaptable tool for assessing and guiding these efforts, providing a lens through which cities can evaluate their progress and refine their approaches. Ultimately, inclusive innovation is not just a policy aspiration but a practical imperative for building resilient, equitable and future-ready urban communities.

5.3 COMMUNITY AGENCY AND ENGAGEMENT

Participants from all four i3o case study cities claim that community participation and meaningful engagement are fundamental to enhancing inclusive innovation via local innovation districts. However, experience shows that not all community participation creates meaningful results and this element is highly challenging to achieve and maintain, precisely because it is a moving target. A common thread across the cities is that the overlap and emphasis on more immediate priorities such as research and commercialisation still renders community engagement as a secondary, rather than a central, element of inclusive innovation.

Newcastle, Pittsburgh and Belfast each struggle to move from "talking the talk" to "walking the walk". Medellín's broader approach of social urbanism creates a more embedded awareness of why it is important to ensure community engagement and participation for enduring social recovery, yet even they struggle to elevate meaningful community engagement. We argue that the city that gets this element right will be poised to become distinct from other innovation districts.

5.3.1 Social urbanism and community engagement in post-conflict contexts

Inclusive innovation in Medellín focused initially on post-violence crisis recovery and now it uses innovation to improve urban life and well-being. The city's approach integrates innovation and spatial interventions in a social urbanism approach to urban transformation that invests in historically marginalised *comunas*. These initiatives use public–private–academic collaborations and engage local communities, reinforcing the idea that innovation must respond to the lived experiences of residents.

From its inception in 2009, Ruta N served as a central node for the city's innovation system from its strategic location in the city's northern zone, a particularly marginalised part of the city. Community engagement is fundamental to Medellín's innovation story and many initiatives actively included engagement in agenda-setting processes, including the surrounding communities in the Northern district, via institutional arrangements with the University–Business–State Committee (CUEE). The participatory ethos of the Medellín model emphasises urban regeneration and mobility projects, creating new opportunities for diverse stakeholders to participate in and contribute to the city's innovation efforts, as well as defining roles and responsibilities for key institutions such as Ruta N.

By contrast, community engagement in Belfast has proven more difficult to materialise at scale. Despite significant work to move beyond the city's legacy of sectarian violence, and some strong examples of project and pilot community innovation exercises, urban transformation in Belfast reveals a city still segregated by class-based urban divisions. The city's fragmentation creates little to no interaction with these neighbourhoods and challenges the ability of workforce development agencies to retrain underemployed youth. Other obstacles include identifying the right community leaders to engage with, managing community gatekeepers, offering long-term and sustainable support, and creating valuable jobs.

Our fieldwork in Belfast gives optimism that effective community engagement is gaining traction in the city due to the presence of committed community-based organisations and supportive public sector and university champions, although Belfast also has a shorter history of pursuing inclusive innovation goals. While policy documents and strategies emphasise social inclusion outcomes as a key objective, specific mentions of public participation are scarce in our discussions with local experts, or in existing policy documents. A persistent concern over the distribution of innovation benefits and the city's economic transformation lingers, and inclusion programmes need to ensure they do not inadvertently disadvantage those they aim to help by creating conflicting eligibility criteria that are at odds with criteria for other social programmes.

5.3.2 Participation in post-industrial contexts

Pittsburgh's economic restructuring created growth-centred strategies linked more to its universities and advanced technology sectors than to the communities left behind by the closure of industrial-era mills. The Greater Hazelwood Neighborhood Plan of 2019[4] includes the design and establishment of the Hazelwood Green Innovation District as part of a wider urban regeneration project, indicating a strong community-centred "North Star Vision" for the area that includes requests for affordable housing, workforce development, post-secondary education for jobs for its residents and the full integration of Hazelwood Green with the community.

For Pittsburgh, these community objectives are at odds with the elite priorities of building a global reputation based on high-technology manufacturing clusters. The greater Hazelwood community highlights a disconnect with the innovation district, exacerbated by the ownership structure of the innovation district that excludes community representation. The reinvention of Hazelwood is challenged by the persistent threat of displacement for long-term residents, and a nagging concern about whether inclusion will be more than window dressing on standard growth-oriented development. At the same time, community residents have proven resistant to supporting infrastructure developments that could enhance connectivity of the innovation district to the wider city; this resistance to change creates suspicion between groups with much to gain from collaboration. Beyond the Hazelwood neighbourhood, the innovation district is recognised as having regional significance, and there is a growing call to identify other priority communities that should be included in Hazelwood Green's outreach and benefit strategies.

Newcastle's narrative is like Pittsburgh's, with the foundational priorities of high-deprivation communities adjacent to the Helix innovation district overlooked in favour of place-making, orthodox STRI results and profit-seeking imperatives from a closed circuit of privileged actors. While the importance of understanding the Newcastle context seems to be recognised by key stakeholders, the make-up and motives driving the role-players in the Helix "coalition" tend to underrepresent the neighbouring communities of Newcastle's West End (the "hosting" local community for Helix) and overlook the surrounding neighbourhoods and the relationships between them. A sustainable and community-focused approach in Newcastle would involve recognising the diversity and mix of activities and institutions that is key to being able to interpret inclusivity and give some consideration to how community outreach can be made meaningful to allow for inclusive outcomes that occur well beyond the district itself (Figure 5.1).

Inclusive innovation is most effective when grounded in the specific assets, challenges and social dynamics of a given territory. Rather than relying on generic engagement models,

Figure 5.1 High-quality place-making in Newcastle's Helix: Newcastle University's Urban Sciences building

place-based inclusive innovation needs to leverage local knowledge, networks and institutions to co-create development strategies tailored to that context. Public participation and community engagement contribute to the contextual relevance and legitimacy of inclusive innovation processes when peripheralised communities and residents have voice in those processes and bring local knowledge into design and implementation. This enhances the social sustainability of innovation efforts and fosters local capacity-building and long-term ownership. Inclusive innovation develops the culture, practice, and processes for economic and social investments that reinforces and support STRI efforts.

5.4 ALIGNING THE INNOVATION ECOSYSTEM TO CITY-REGION PRIORITIES

The third component of inclusive innovation emerging from the four case studies is that it is important to align innovation district goals to the broader territorial strategies of the city-region. This is a call for *policy* inclusion that is just as vital as *physical* and *social* inclusion, so that the work incubated within the innovation district and the city's broader innovation ecosystem attracts and maintains broad political and business support. This aligns with Katz and Wagner's recognition that collaborative leadership networks matter *within* innovation districts,[5] extending it to emphasise how important policy links *beyond* the innovation district are to encourage overall regional progress.

Building links between innovation district goals and broader regional policies and strategies will expand the coalition that cares about the success of inclusive innovation. Possibly the biggest inclusive innovation challenge for innovation districts is avoiding the "crowding-out" of inclusion priorities by other legitimate goals that can occupy the time of even the most high-capacity district management team – tasks including research, innovation, commercialisation, property development, environmental sustainability and financial stewardship, to name but a few. These are all necessary priorities, but they need to be framed in ways that matter to regional stakeholders beyond the district.

In Newcastle, for example, the public-sector leadership of the Helix champions inclusive growth and makes it an explicit target for broader regional policy. Priority intervention strategies include addressing child poverty, reducing health inequalities, widening access to skills and employment pathways to "good jobs", addressing digital and social exclusion, integrating health skills and housing ecosystems, supporting business growth in priority technological sectors, and also productivity and good work growth in foundation sectors, and fostering local participation (to prevent gentrification and displacement). These intentional links between district-scale performance benchmarking and regional policy goals create greater incentive for policymakers to pay attention to what is occurring within the innovation district. Similarly,

Medellín is widely recognised for its robust and innovative approach to what is often termed "social urbanism" or "social innovation". The city's transformation from a highly violent and unequal place in the 1980s–90s to a lauded model of urban innovation is deeply rooted in this strategy, which uses architecture, infrastructure, culture, and education as tools for social inclusion and economic development, targeting historically marginalised communities. The core idea is to integrate these peripheral areas, often informal settlements on hillsides (see Figure 4.6), into the formal city fabric and provide residents with access to opportunities and services.

Belfast resembles Newcastle in terms of its clear city strategies,[6] including the Belfast Agenda (which incorporates an explicit Inclusive Growth Strategy),[7] the Northern Ireland government's economic vision[8] (in which Belfast plays a major role), and a partnership Belfast City Region Deal.[9] Each policy document embeds an STRI strategy at the heart of reinvention, whilst emphasising the requirement for inclusive approaches to local communities previously involved in and separated by the Troubles. Each document has its own suite of targets and performance metrics for measuring progress, which can be adapted to provide inclusive innovation dashboards for the innovation districts and major role players.

The challenge for Belfast's innovation ecosystem is that the city-region's innovation hubs are spatially dispersed, aside from the Harbour Board's Titanic Quarter, which almost acts as a separate district adjacent to the city (see Figure 4.4). There is a case for Innovation City Belfast (ICB) to convene and synthesise these strategies and the performance management of their delivery.[10] As the capital of Northern Ireland, Belfast needs to take the lead in defining and managing its impact on inclusion agendas across Northern Ireland.

Pittsburgh is another example of a city that needs to consider a tighter definition of its inclusion goals, and how the activities occurring within the Hazelwood Green innovation district align to the broader innovation ecosystem that includes Pittsburgh Innovation District (in the heart of the university precinct in Oakland) and that lacks clear guidance from the public sector, and an apparent lack of support from the state. For instance, a previous city administration adopted a high-profile Roadmap for Inclusive Innovation in 2015,[11] whose spreadsheets were still being serviced up to at least 2023. Yet in three wide-ranging study visits to the city, this plan was never referred to by anyone interviewed for the i3o project.

This fragmentation is exacerbated by the long history of the Hazelwood Green innovation district. Its development pathways and approaches to inclusive innovation are essentially determined by the three philanthropic foundation owners. This has provided the benefits of patient capital and considerable resource adequacy for getting the universities and other occupiers on board. What has been almost absent has been strategic alignment and territorial equity discussions of the inclusion consequences of creating a hub of global quality and national significance in this location, even though it is near both the city centre and the university precinct and Pittsburgh Innovation District.

Innovation district intervention strategies should contribute to wider local and regional inclusive growth strategies and plans, and take their potential city-region and regional impacts seriously. Their leadership and management need to engage with other relevant growth and development "ecosystems" (e.g., enterprise, employment, education and skills, social cohesion). They should seek to explore and agree on how their policies and practice contributes to how the overall city and city-region works, and strengthen their impact on inclusion priorities locally and regionally.

5.5 CALIBRATING THE MIX: APPROACHING INNOVATION DISTRICTS 2.0

The international comparative analysis of innovation districts conducted by the i3o project finds strong evidence that these post-industrial, post-conflict cities are making intentional efforts to forge new urban futures based on STRI investments in urban innovation districts that position inclusive innovation goals at the forefront of their planning and execution. While none of the four cases represents a perfect model for other districts to emulate, three elements are apparent across them that indicate an active and evolving process to create an Innovation District 2.0 that transcends the narrowly circumscribed criteria for success that traditional urban innovation districts represent. Beyond occupancy rates, land value, job creation and urban narratives is emerging a new set of opportunities that are foregrounded in addressing broader societal goals and therefore enhancing and expanding the benefits arising from initial public investments in these sites for innovation. The three elements that each city is working to enhance are *leadership*, *engagement* and *alignment*. No element can be separated from the other two, and in the final Chapter 6 we conclude by recommending how these cities, and others, can work to win the race to attaining a new standard in innovation district outcomes.

NOTES

1 Lee N (2023) Inclusive innovation in cities: From buzzword to policy. *Regional Studies*, 59(1): 2168637. https://doi.org/10.1080/00343404.2023.2168637

2 Hambleton R (2019) The new civic leadership: Place and the co-creation of public innovation. *Public Money & Management*, 39(4): 271–279. https://doi.org/10.1080/09540962.2019.1592908; Kneale D, Stansfield C, Goldman R, Lester S, Edwards RC and Thomas J (2024) The implementation of embedded researchers in policy, public services, and commercial settings: A systematic evidence and gap map. *Implementation Science Communications*, 5(1): 41. https://doi.org/10.1186/s43058-024-00570-3

3 Morales D, Green L, Marlow M, Cadena Gaitán C, Deitrick S, Glass MR and Kempton L (2025) Defining inclusive innovation: Challenges and lessons for innovation districts. *Regional Studies, Regional Science*, 12(1): 740–753. https://doi.org/10.1080/21681376.2025.2543915

4 City of Pittsburgh (2019) *Greater Hazelwood Neighbourhood Plan*. https://engage.pittsburghpa.gov/greater-hazelwood-neighborhood-plan

5 Katz B and Wagner J (2014) *The Rise of Innovation Districts: A New Geography of Innovation in America*. Washington, DC: Brookings Institution Metropolitan Policy Program.

6 See https://www.belfastcity.gov.uk/council/our-strategies

7 See https://www.belfastcity.gov.uk/Documents/Our-commitment-to-Inclusive-Growth-2020-2022; City of Belfast (2024) *The Belfast Agenda*. https://www.belfastcity.gov.uk/Community/Community-planning/Belfast-Agenda

8 Department for the Economy (2021) *10× Economy – An Economic Vision*. https://www.economy-ni.gov.uk/articles/10x-economy-economic-vision

9 See https://belfastregioncitydeal.co.uk/; UK Government (2019) *Belfast Region City Deal*. https://assets.publishing.service.gov.uk/media/5c9a008fe5274a3ca24460c3/HoT-_City_Deals-_Final_-_with_signatures__1_.pdf

10 ICB, a partnership between Belfast City Council, Belfast Harbour, Catalyst, Queen's University and Ulster University, aims to stimulate collaboration and innovation among business, academic, government and community participants.

11 SSTI (2015) *Pittsburgh Launches Inclusive Innovation Roadmap to Support Equitable Access to Technology, City Resources, Information*. ion | SSTI. https://ssti.org/blog/pittsburgh-launches-inclusive-innovation-roadmap-support-equitable-access-technology-city

6. Policy and practice insights for innovation districts

6.1 INTRODUCTION

This Policy Impact book addresses how inclusive innovation is becoming central to the evolution of science, technology and research-led innovation (STRI) in four cities that are transitioning away from legacies that impacted their economic development trajectory. By pairing two post-industrial cities – Newcastle (UK) and Pittsburgh (USA) – and two post-conflict cities – Belfast (UK) and Medellín (Colombia) – the book provides a city typology that will be recognisable in other cities and regions, yet all four cities are more complex and multidimensional than these labels might suggest.

Two of the cases (Belfast and Medellín) faced redevelopment challenges caused by their legacy of structural urban violence. All four cases can be considered as "post-industrial" cities to some extent, though this is most profound for Newcastle and Pittsburgh, both representing the North Atlantic narrative of painful deindustrialisation and gradual rebirth. All four cities use the promise of STRI to catalyse regional economic restructuring, and each features an innovation ecosystem that is moving beyond classic indicators of innovation-led success. There is a drive and commitment in each place to build a new type of urban-focused innovation district that avoids the social and spatial inequalities that characterise traditional innovation districts. Adding explicit inclusion goals represents the latest evolution for innovation ecosystems and we predict that the city-regions successfully navigating the transition to an Innovation District 2.0 model will optimise their impact, ultimately leading to greater outcomes from their initial investments.

The four cases have some potential to inform other post-industrial and post-conflict STRI-based reinvention journeys; to ambitious cities in the Global North and Global South; to national contexts where innovation district investments are predominantly nationally driven (as in the UK), or where they are led by regional stakeholders (as in Medellín and Belfast) or led by local philanthropic foundations (as we found in Pittsburgh). The cases also span cities that are growing very rapidly, and those seeking to converge with faster growing places in population and economic terms.

Our research demonstrates that a new model of innovation district is emerging that can address societal challenges through inclusive innovation. We find that innovation districts need to consider wider issues of alignment and territorial equity, especially if:

- they are big enough to have city and even regional impact;
- their development creates risks of displacement and other negative effects; and
- there are opportunities for the innovation district to create positive change.

Local culture and context are critical to explaining how the development stories of each case study unfolded; yet each faces similar inclusive innovation challenges and they share

https://doi.org/10.1080/2578711X.2025.2624329

potential solutions that can be adopted by other cities. The Improving Inclusive Innovation Outcomes (i3o) project designed and used a set of diagnostic tools through a multi-year process involving repeated interactions with the case cities. In each case desk research and preliminary case study research were followed by fieldwork that brought together insights from participants across the cities' innovation ecosystems, as well as experts and intermediaries who were impacted by STRI-based development policies. This included community partners and academic experts as well as representatives from the public, private and non-profit sectors.

Each city has followed distinctive pathways to designing and operating urban innovation districts. In the two post-conflict cities, inclusion considerations have always had some prominence. Urban reinvention needed to address social cohesion as part of the strategy for reducing the risk of renewed violence. The post-industrial cities of Newcastle and Pittsburgh have balanced their capability to host an internationally recognisable competitive innovation district model with inclusive growth ambitions. In Pittsburgh, the focus on the immediately adjacent residential community to Hazelwood Green has come at the detriment of considering the wider city and city-region inclusion impacts. Newcastle has evolved towards a city-inclusive growth concern, yet it underplays the impacts it will have on the immediate adjacent West End community. All four districts and innovation ecosystems are evolving towards something novel because of the local presence of inclusion champions who recognise the prospective benefits of creating social and economic impacts beyond the narrow set of stakeholders directly involved in the innovation district.

In this final chapter, we underscore the key findings from our project with a range of actionable recommendations drawn from the four case study sites. The three key elements of effective leadership, community engagement and strategic alignment can be replicated by other innovation districts regardless if they are already operational or just in the planning stages. Fundamental in any case is making sure that consequential community representation is embedded in the governance and strategic planning of innovation districts that want to be considered inclusive.

6.2 KEY INSIGHTS FOR IMPROVING INCLUSIVE INNOVATION OUTCOMES

The i3o project engaged with four urban innovation ecosystems representing two types of city-regions: those facing transitions from a past reliance on industrial production and those emerging from conditions of structural violence. We found that the coalition of stakeholders involved in innovation district development varied across the four cities, with each led by different sectoral leadership structures (for details, see Chapter 4). Each city was shifting toward inclusive innovation goals as central components of their STRI and wider inclusive growth strategies. In Newcastle, a coalition of local government and research university leadership came together to create the Helix, where proximity to historically less-advantaged communities creates a visible contrast to the national "centres of excellence" located on the site. Pittsburgh's public sector is notably absent from planning of the city's Hazelwood Green innovation district, where a coalition of philanthropic organisations is supported by the city's two major research universities in revitalising a former brownfield site. Medellín's role as Colombia's innovation hub and most globally connected city means that federal, state and local governments are integrated in planning for the Ruta N site. The build-out from the Titanic Quarter of Belfast's innovation ecosystem, and plans for a polycentric innovation district, are increasingly led by the Innovation City Belfast (ICB) partnership, anchored by the reestablished devolved Northern Ireland government, Belfast City Council and local universities.

Each city's innovation district is at a different stage of maturation, with Ruta N and the Helix more advanced than the Hazelwood Green or Belfast's emerging ICB sites. The experience of each city in pursuing inclusion as a centrepiece of its planning goals indicates three core elements that other city-regions could follow to enhance their innovation strategies to deliver strong results based on public investments.

- *Leadership and management matters*

  It was apparent that leaders in each city could explain why inclusion represents a non-partisan opportunity to enhance the spillover effects arising from innovation district development. Newcastle's existing innovation district leadership team, and the city's anticipated "Health Innovation Neighborhood" (HIN), are continuing to use i3o tools to ensure that inclusion goals become part of the overall leadership framework for future innovation district planning. Belfast's nascent innovation ecosystem is considering ways to streamline inclusive innovation leadership within the planned ICB strategies.

- *Community engagement and place-making is vital*

  Community representation and "buy in" to places that function integrally as part of the local and city urban systems are necessary predicates for making sure that innovation districts do not become (or continue to function as) exclusive enclaves for universities and high-technology firms and instead deliver opportunities for communities: either in the form of products and services, or via employment and engagement. Creating accessible, multi-use neighbourhoods and venues for urban life is critical. In Pittsburgh there is great appetite for more conversation and clarity about what the new Hazelwood Green innovation district will mean for nearby residents and firms, as a new mixed-use residential community, and as a destination for a breadth of city activity.

- *Strategic alignment and territorial equity are fundamental*

  If innovation district strategies are not a key component of wider urban and regional planning objectives, then the chances to enhance spillovers from innovation district policy will fail.

Medellín has an emerging need to clarify the district's inclusion and social value policies to revised national policies and to the calls for greater regional inclusion that account for disparities in opportunity between the city of Medellín, its metropolitan hinterland and the broader province of Antioquia.

6.3 COMMUNITY REPRESENTATION: THE MISSING LINK

The challenge for innovation districts internationally is how to build a valid model to include community representation and a sense of agency within their strategic planning and tactical management. Part of this challenge is simply experiential: there is less familiarity with sustained and sincere community engagement on the part of land developers and other innovation district developers.

There are emerging efforts in many cities to adopt "inclusive growth" strategies as their approach to develop and embed new forms of co-creation and participatory governance in their planning. In Newcastle, Pittsburgh and Belfast, the land and property development industries that design and deliver innovation district schemes have too often been most familiar with planning-based regulations and compliance-based community engagement regimes, and are only beginning to shift toward meaningful community representation.

In contexts such as the United States, community benefits agreements are a common way to ensure that land development meets local community needs, through legal arrangements that provide employment opportunities for local residents, or that provide for investments in affordable housing or new public spaces as part of the negotiation about urban redevelopment. A significant problem with these agreements is that they tend to be highly transactional in nature. Rather than functioning as reciprocal or living documents that provide sustained benefits to all signatories, they tend to provide benefits to comparatively limited local populations, with a single community-based organisation given lobbying authority that might exclude other resident priorities. Our research calls for a different approach, where the externalities from innovation districts are developed in concert with district leadership, communities and businesses.

In the UK context, the planning systems of both Newcastle and Belfast require mandatory community involvement processes. Both the councils and universities will typically adopt and implement extensive community engagement strategies. However, both cities recognise that inclusive growth in general, and innovation districts in particular, need to go well beyond the statutory minimum. There is now specific intent to embed and sustain community involvement more deeply in the new Health Innovation Neighbourhood in Newcastle from its origin. In Belfast, ICB is committed to systematically augmenting community representation and involvement as the institution evolves.

In Medellín, the commitment to a social urbanism ethos has sought community engagement in STRI growth as a fundamental principle. Mechanisms such as participatory budgeting for resource allocation and comprehensive urban projects for physical and social development have sought to ensure that citizens are not just recipients of innovation, but active co-creators of the city's transformation. The ongoing challenge is for innovation district participants to adapt and evolve in the face of the continuing influx of new communities to the city-region from both internal and international migration.

6.4 RECOMMENDATIONS FOR LOCAL AND REGIONAL POLICY

The research conducted on inclusive innovation strategies in the four case cities indicates that leadership and management; proactive community engagement and place-making; and strategic alignment and territorial equity are the key elements for urban innovation district stakeholders who want to overcome the limits of the Innovation District 1.0 model that overlooks the prospect of maximising benefits from these large-scale investments for the wider city-region, its communities and local micro and small businesses.

Based on interviews, document reviews and policy roundtables conducted in the four cities and informed by an academic and policy literature that exists on innovation district evolution, we offer policy insights for city and regional leadership teams to consider in order to enhance the social and economic benefits that can arise from investment in innovation districts. There is room to adapt these recommendations to local conditions, and the foremost finding from our research is that place continues to matter even as innovation districts inherently operate toward national and global scales.

Our differentiation of what we term the Innovation District 1.0 and an Innovation District 2.0 framework is presented in summary in Figure 6.1.

6.4.1 Inclusive innovation with leadership and management

INSIGHT 1: PURPOSEFULNESS

- Leadership coalitions must be clearly identifiable and have a shared sense of the value-added nature of inclusive innovation for their place

Innovation districts are significant investments in place that will make important contributions to urban development trajectories over extended periods. Given how significant this investment will be for intergenerational transformation of formerly disinvested areas, leadership coalitions must be clearly identifiable and accountable for both the positive and negative spillover effects that the innovation district will cause. *Innovation district leadership teams*

Figure 6.1 Distinctions between the Innovation District 1.0 and Innovation District 2.0 models

Actionable i3o Insight	Innovation District Orthodoxy	Innovation Districts 2.0
Leadership and Management	Focused on aggregate economic, commercial, financial, and innovation goals Overly reliant on incidental trickle-down impacts for inclusion	Holds a purposeful inclusive innovation vision and priorities
		Embedded in business planning and performance management
		Proactive curation of innovation district tenants and activities
		Agreed degrees of community agency
Community Engagement and Placemaking	Innovation district management and tenants look inwards, creating a pleasant place for tenants, innovation district activities and networks, but ignoring neighbouring communities	Inclusive, outward-looking placemaking that invites active participation
		Addressing local societal challenges
		Seeking quick wins to build local confidence
		Balancing local needs with wider left-behind communities
Strategic Alignment and Territorial Equity	Governance and strategy creates a self-contained enclave and ecosystem that is not linked to other relevant city-region strategies	Seeks distinct contributions to city-region inclusive growth and other relevant strategies
		Considers how the innovation district can influence other towns and neighbourhoods of the city-region

should regularly discuss, agree, and share their explicit inclusive innovation purposes and priorities. The composition of a leadership coalition will vary from city to city, yet it is important that innovation district compacts stipulate who holds responsibility for setting and maintaining the district's strategic vision. This coalition must hold clear roles for the relevant municipalities as the legitimate, accountable stewards of place and most often democratic representatives of local populations.

Regardless of its leadership structure, the leadership group must hold a clear sense of the value-added nature of inclusive innovation if the benefits of Innovation Districts 2.0 are to be realised. The value proposition for inclusive innovation is best codified through ownership documents, tenancy agreements and in any site planning that occurs.

INSIGHT 2: BUSINESS PLANNING

- Innovation districts must create place-sensitive indicators that monitor how STRI benefits are distributed beyond the boundaries of the district

Having agreed explicit inclusive innovation purposes, innovation district leadership teams need to agree on the delivery plans to achieve them and include them in their overall district plans. Inclusive innovation goals and objectives can be managed and reviewed with a similar rigour to other dimensions of the district's business plans. Monitoring should exceed standard measures of economic development performance (such as occupancy rates or land value capture) and evolve to develop indicators that identify how the benefits of STRI are distributed beyond the geographical boundaries of the district, creating inclusionary outcomes that include workforce participation and training, localisation of supply chains, community procurement activities, and entrepreneurship opportunities.

INSIGHT 3: CURATION

- Leadership should strive for a tenancy mix that encourages inclusive innovation within and beyond the innovation district

Innovation district leadership should be bold and intentional about calibrating the mix of tenants, activities and networks that can foster inclusive innovation within and beyond the district. Active intervention is necessary because innovation districts are frequently embedded in areas with challenging development histories – this means that a singular focus on occupancy rates could deepen inequalities and exclusion, simply because of the investment gap between the district and the surrounding neighbourhood. As we explain throughout this book, the challenge of embedding social value and inclusion to broaden the impact of place-based investments means determining a plan to interact and integrate the innovation district with the broader city and its innovation ecosystem. This could mean bringing in public spaces, workforce training or housing that attracts residents into the innovation district, as well as seeking business tenants that add value and intention to the strategic goals of the district.

INSIGHT 4: COMMUNITY AGENCY

- Leadership should come to a consensus with relevant communities of place and interest about how they should be engaged in planning and managing the district

Innovation districts should be spaces where adjacent communities have a sense of pride and ownership in what is being created. Orthodox STRI-based purposes are essential to the success of innovation districts, yet Innovation District 2.0 models can co-design processes with local communities to reach a consensus on the features that benefit the maximum possible range of stakeholders. Co-designed principles and practices in district leadership and management (including formal governance and advisory structures, and business planning and review processes) build legitimacy and relevance for the innovation district. This empowered community agency will help Innovation District 2.0 leaders to "walking the walk" of inclusive innovation.

6.4.2 Community engagement and place-making

INSIGHT 5: INCLUSIVE PLACE-MAKING

- Include co-designing welcoming spaces, transport, and housing that are accessible to local communities and the wider city

The primary challenge for innovation districts is to make them appealing to potential investors and occupiers. This remains critical, but Innovation Districts 2.0 need to couple this with creating a mixed-use neighbourhood and city destination. An Innovation District 2.0 appreciates its role and function as part of the broader urban fabric of the city as much as creating high-quality amenities for its tenants and their activities. Co-designing the animation and accessibility of relevant parts of the district with local communities and business will give physical representation to the challenges of agency and local ownership highlighted above in Insight 4.

INSIGHT 6: ADDRESS SOCIAL CHALLENGES

- Encourage projects and programmes that improve the experiences and opportunities for local communities and businesses

An Innovation District 2.0 should be aware of the major societal challenges that confront local and city communities of place and interest. They can look for and encourage win–wins where their tenants and activities contribute to major local social, economic and environmental challenges and are tackled. Innovation Districts 2.0 can create processes identifying how district programmes can assist in addressing these challenges, and leadership structures should facilitate knowledge transfer out of the innovation district to provide material benefits to surrounding communities. Test-bedding innovations that are of prospective assistance to residents and firms in the adjacent area can foster a sense of inclusion by demonstrating that there are tangible local benefits from STRI.

INSIGHT 7: SHORT-TERM WINS

- Deliver short-term wins that build local confidence in, and a commitment to, the generational vision and profound changes a successful district will entail

Innovation district formation and evolution is a long-term endeavour fundamentally at odds with family and community time scales. It is unrealistic and counter-productive to suggest that community residents will receive immediate or short-term benefits from new innovation districts. Inclusion involves a candid and realistic accounting for the long-term build-up needed by innovation districts to achieve viable social results. This realism will engender less cynicism from surrounding communities than if unrealistic promises are made regarding the nature of the workforce opportunities or community benefits arising from the districts.

A tangible way that innovation districts can deliver short-term impacts to their communities is by investing in and animating high-quality public spaces, public transit and sustainable transport access, and diverse housing options to ensure the district is genuinely welcoming to local and regional talent and diverse residents. Simultaneously, they can consider how local business, social enterprise and community uses can be accommodated within parts of the district, establish local job creation and educational programmes, making the district a tangible source of pride and opportunity for the community, not just a segregated economic enclave.

INSIGHT 8: BALANCING PERSPECTIVES AND PRIORITIES

- Inclusive innovation involves the co-creation of new ideas, practices or technologies with local communities, businesses and organisations to address societal challenges, ensuring equitable benefit distribution and fostering community empowerment

The goal of inclusive innovation is hence one of maximising regional impacts from the activities occurring in a narrowly defined site. A prospective limiting factor to large-scale spillover effects is if hyper-local concerns are the only communities of place and interests who are involved in the determination of inclusive innovation goals and priorities.

Community engagement should proactively engage adjacent neighbourhoods. The most ambitious Innovation Districts 2.0 can go beyond a compensatory, corporate social responsibility approach to adjacent communities. Community engagement structures should consider how civil society actors, labour groups and private sector interests across the city-region can be involved. Innovation district governance and management should provide an oversight structure that encourages the benefits of STRI activity in the innovation district to extend beyond the district's boundaries. It should foster a collective sense of community ownership and understanding about the activities occurring within the innovation district in the wider city-region. There is a balance to be struck between a focus on adjacent neighbourhoods and other vulnerable communities in the wider city-region.

6.4.3 Territorial equity and strategic alignment

INSIGHT 9: ALIGNMENT MATTERS

- Ensure innovation district policy is coherent with broader regional plans

Innovation districts should not develop counter to or in isolation from other plans for regional economic development. Inclusion goals should include territorial inclusiveness by fostering a sense of alignment with other regional plans. This requires greater coordination with local and regional governments and an appreciation for how to shape the activities occurring in the district to create complementary relationships to other economic development activities. Innovation districts should discuss the balance between activities and outcomes designed primarily with and for adjacent communities, and the wider impacts that can be delivered by Innovation Districts 2.0 for disadvantaged and vulnerable groups in the wider city and region. At a very practical level, this might involve innovation districts assuming degrees of leadership and accountability for specific elements of inclusion-oriented goals and activities in relevant city strategies.

INSIGHT 10: TERRITORIAL EQUITY AWARENESS

- Promote an awareness of and manage how the innovation district's spatial, economic, and social impacts shape the territorial development pathways of urban centres and other places in the wider city-region

Larger innovation districts will have major impacts on the development trajectories of the whole region. They attract investment and will shape the location of higher value jobs, transport patterns and where people live to access those jobs. Innovation District 2.0 leadership teams should work with city-region partners to consider their impact on territorial development throughout the city and region.

This links to the other insights: look outwards as well as inwards and manage these outward externalities. Policies such as rapid transit, education and supply chain outreach, and property market management are part of the in-scope discussions to be had as part of optimising strategic alignment with inclusive growth and other relevant strategies. The future Innovation District 2.0 will be part of wider urban ecosystems – innovation certainly, but also skills, employment, property market, residential and others as appropriate.

6.5 TOWARD INNOVATION DISTRICTS 2.0

While innovation districts are a global phenomenon and have a set of universal best practices, we argue that a strengths-based approach to innovation district formation that leverages local culture, identity and economic assets will provide a more sustainable model for economic development than pure replication of models from elsewhere. This means that instead of replicating elements of international innovation districts, the leadership teams of each district should instead remember to benefit from locally specific strengths and attributes to differentiate themselves from other districts. Innovation District 2.0 exemplars will have anchor institution and investment partners capable of explaining why focusing on inclusion is good for places and communities – not by describing the generic intent of inclusive innovation, but by explaining why *your* innovation district's focus is good for your city and region.

The overall goal of the i3o project is to assist city and city-region coalitions to achieve urban economic redevelopment that overcome past approaches that, whether or not intentionally, tended to restrict the benefits of innovation-led growth. There is a historical tendency toward focusing inward within innovation districts, with the focus on securing development *within* the site to the exclusion of strategies that will maximise benefits *inclusively* to populations and neighbourhoods beyond the immediate boundaries of the district. The new leaders in place-based innovation will undoubtedly be those who achieve this transition, unleashing the capacity of innovation to bring about economic and social benefits by connecting with the people, places and organisations that are one or more steps removed from the often-cloistered confines of the innovation district.

Our work in Colombia, the UK and United States shows that innovation districts are continuing to evolve, and that tentative moves are beginning that are taking inclusion seriously as a central component of what we are coining as "Innovation Districts 2.0". This new model of innovation district will transcend geographical demarcations of where the investments have occurred and instead stretch outward, actively involving communities and companies that are looking to engage in the city's innovation ecosystem. Inclusive innovation is about amplifying the spillover effects from place-based investments in former brownfield sites by adopting the position of strategic impatience: not waiting for full occupancy rates within the district's confines but instead reaching out to encourage a diverse set of firms and communities to engage with the ideas of urban transformation that each innovation district represents.

Future phases of the i3o programme will expand the number of study sites to evaluate whether other tendencies toward a new Innovation District 2.0 model are evident. However, at this point the emergent paradigm seems to consist of the following features:

- Innovation Districts 2.0 will develop STRI leadership teams who embrace inclusive innovation as a central component of their vision and values, and can operationalise this through strategic planning and operations management by nurturing relationships to deliver more inclusion-rich innovation within and beyond the confines of each innovation district.
- Innovation Districts 2.0 will counter enclave development through encouraging physical and social access to the resources located in each site, by animating their public spaces in ways that encourage everyone to feel part of the activities occurring there, and that have accountable leadership teams that participate in neighbourhood, city and regional planning – especially if residential developments are envisaged as part of innovation district planning.
- Innovation Districts 2.0 will contribute to wider local and regional inclusive growth strategies and plans by taking their responsibility to enhancing potential city-region and regional impacts seriously.

6.6 CONCLUSIONS

This Policy Impact book's genesis was a very local and very specific observation stimulated by wandering past "The People's Kitchen" as you enter the shiny new precinct of the Helix innovation district in Newcastle's city centre: How does the Helix innovation district positively affect the experience and opportunities of those people who receive hot food, friendship and support from The People's Kitchen?

This book concludes with a call for an Innovation District 2.0 model, literally globally, that can answer the origin question, and its local variants in other places, much more positively than was attained by now-standard Innovation District 1.0 examples. The challenge to shift paradigms is needed more than ever in what seems to be a particularly polarised and divisive period for local, regional and national economic development.

The i3o methodology and toolkit, tested in and developed by the four participating cities, appears to offer one approach to designing and developing more inclusion-rich Innovation District 2.0 models that might work in places worldwide. It illustrates how places in general, and innovation districts in particular, can define inclusive innovation and thereafter diagnose and develop how they are going to deliver it more effectively.

A global programme needs additional and different role players. The four cities are an emergent community of practice that will welcome new partners and participants. Alongside new models of innovation district, i3o is also a new way of conducting academic–policy exchange – long-term, interdisciplinary, and framed by the context and culture of the participating cities, and hopefully by their communities, as much as by the requirements of their universities and research ecosystems.

Transitions to an Innovation District 2.0 model can also serve as a template for other orthodox economic growth strategies, from both the STRI and urban renewal perspectives. Further adaptation will be required, but major innovation programmes hosted by other institutions can apply an i3o-type of lens to how they address their inclusion impacts.

Moving beyond designated innovation districts to the plethora of area-based initiatives – freeports, opportunity and investment zones, knowledge quarters, even new towns and garden villages – might benefit from new methodologies and toolkits that can read-across to innovation districts. And beyond formal area-based initiatives, why would not any large campuses – university, new industries, tech and data, among others – adapt and adopt tools, techniques, and some variants of academic–policy exchange that might draw on the lessons learned from pioneering innovation districts?

In conclusion, this book seeks to offer a foundational Innovation District 2.0 framework for policymakers globally. The insights – leveraged from the unique challenges of four post-industrial and post-conflict cities – demonstrate that intentional, inclusion-oriented policy design is not a secondary objective but can be a core driver of successful innovation ecosystems.

Moving forward, we urge policymakers to consider this methodology, to systematically embed social cohesion and accessibility from the inception of innovation district development strategies, and perhaps for wider initiatives. We believe this work opens fertile ground for future research and development: a shift from pondering whether we can define inclusive innovation to exploring which specific inclusion policies generate more equitable spatial, social, and economic outcomes through intense and enduring academic–policy exchange.

Those readers who are up for either or both challenges will be welcome in the i3o community of practice. We hope you will be part of taking forward these important areas of practical work and enquiry.

For Product Safety Concerns and Information please contact our EU representative GPSR@taylorandfrancis.com Taylor & Francis Verlag GmbH, Kaufingerstraße 24, 80331 München, Germany

Batch number: 10761701

Printed by Printforce, the Netherlands